Flower Embroidery

Flower Embroidery

by

Allianora Rosse

Photography by Rosanna H. Rosse

Charles Scribner's Sons
New York

Copyright © 1975 Allianora Rosse

Library of Congress Cataloging in Publication Data

Rosse, Allianora.
    Flower embroidery.
    1. Embroidery—Patterns.   2. Design, Decorative—

Plant forms.   I. Title.
TT773.R66   746.4′4   74-13063
ISBN 0-684-14013-6

All embroideries and their illustrations are
by the author

1 3 5 7 9 11 13 15 17 19 C/MD 20 18 16 14 12 10 8 6 4 2

Printed in the United States of America

DEDICATION

To my mother
S. HELENA ROSSE
who instilled in me the
love of flowers and
embroidery, and who
inspired me to do this
book

Contents

Flower Embroidery

Preface

As a young child, I saw much embroidery about the house. Not only were there many examples of antique and ethnic embroidery in the form of pillows, collars, knitting bags, and much more, but also my father, who was a many-sided designer, had great interest in the whole William Morris movement, consequently in embroidery, which was one of the media used for many of the William Morris designs. As a young man, my father created several designs in the Peace Palace in The Hague, Holland. One of these was a frieze of appliqué embroidery around one of the court rooms. Another influence was my seeing and admiring many beautiful flower embroideries in several copies of the old British Embroiderer's Guild magazine, which he had in his collection.

A gifted artist, my mother never got around to doing much embroidery because of her large family. She was a garden designer first and foremost, and such time that wasn't spent on the family was spent on that. But she loves embroidery and has collected many exquisite examples through the years. The desire to do such embroidery has stayed with me throughout my life.

The floral embroideries in the embroidery magazines influenced my whole career as an artist. Not only did I specialize in flowers, but also I think that my composition and style have always had embroidery possibilities. My textile designs were definitely influenced by embroidery, and now in this book I am reversing the process. Many of the textile designs are being adapted to the designs in this book.

It is my intention to give the reader how-to guidance with respect to floral embroidery. I also want to stress the realistic look rather than the fantastic. So much has already been written, taught, and demonstrated about unrealistic flowers. Crewel designs are in essence fantasy, and purely decorative. I definitely do not exclude the decorative —and therefore sometimes geometric and stylized—side of embroidered flowers, but I feel realistic flowers can have all these characteristics too. Actually, I use yarn and thread and materials as media to depict flowers.

My embroidery pieces are not made for competition. I do not pretend to be an embroidery expert. Experts might argue with my stitches and methods; they could criticize the way I finish off the back of an embroidery. I may go against the rules, but I feel that as long as the end results are satisfying and beautiful, who will know or care what the back of the work looks like? I admire the fine reverse work of old embroideries, but I also feel that until now only a very few people looked at the reverse. I don't recommend sloppiness, however. Embroiderers should work their designs in the way most pleasing to themselves to achieve the effect desired.

As for the use of frames, it is extremely difficult for me to make a neat, flat embroidery without a frame. In a few instances, such as when cross-stitching on a firm background, I seldom use one. But if the background material is supple and easily pulled out of shape, a frame of some kind is needed even for cross-stitching. True, using a frame is not always easy, but the end results are definitely better and easier to handle.

This book is not written for beginners. The reader should be quite experienced and familiar with embroidery to be able to follow my instructions, as I will not deal with the making of specific stitches or the threading of needles. My purpose is to inspire a wider and artistically more effective use of flowers in embroidery, and to give a description of my methods for producing that result.

I have always loved embroidering, and I have always loved flowers. I hope it will be possible to describe in this book how I have brought the two together.

A full list of the botanical species shown in the embroideries will be found on page 80.

A General Approach to Flower Embroidery

Flower embroidery has a very long history. On the fragile remnants of a Coptic robe one can clearly see flower embroidery consisting of tapestry-weave tulips in needle-weave stitch. The ancient Persians, Chinese, Japanese, and many other ethnic groups used flowers as part of their embroidery. As civilization progressed, flowers generally maintained a very important place in all sorts of decoration and design and consequently also in embroidery. In many countries where embroidery still played a part in clothing decoration, flowers were used with great frequency and in hues ranging from the natural to the fantastic.

Almost all floral embroidery was and is stylized and decorative. Some is not only stylized and decorative but also forthrightly fanciful. Not only in their general impression could such floral designs be described as such, but individually the flowers were the furthest thing from being realistic or natural looking.

Of course, there are many reasons why flowers evolved this way in embroidery. Probably the fashions and fads of the day or era had the strongest influence on how they were depicted in embroidery. National tradition also played a part: the same patterns and designs were handed down from generation to generation.

When wall-hangings in the shape of tapestries were used to keep the dank cold of castle walls to a minimum, it was stylish to have hangings that portrayed pleasant outdoor scenes. Very many of the early European tapestries showed such romantic scenes as sweet dam-

The head of Flora
in Botticelli's *Primavera*

sels in distress, or gallant and elegant gentlemen enjoying the hunt, or other then acceptable pastimes. Here we almost always have a few figures of humans and animals gracefully placed amongst various plants and shrubs in what, I suppose, could be called gardens. Some of the plants are clearly recognizable as very common wild flowers or basic species of present-day flora. As a matter of fact, the old tapestries are still a good source of information as to what grew in the gardens and forests of those days. I take the tapestries as an example because to me embroidery and tapestry weaving are not far removed, and indeed, some old tapestries offer very suitable designs for embroidery.

Looking for other examples of how flowers and plant material have been used in embroidery through the centuries, the gourd comes to mind. In ancient Persia the gourd was the symbol of fertility. But a gourd is a gourd, and, I suppose, after working a plain gourd into their designs for some time, people felt the need to doodle and frill the original motif. And if this was the way it developed, it was easy to elaborate and glorify and stylize. It was that way in their painting and weaving, and consequently in due course we were given the celebrated paisley design, which also occurred in their embroidery.*

How pleasing and simple a design to manipulate in such a way! It certainly has been a durable motif; no other plant has ever been so glorified. However, I can't help thinking that a realistic treatment of the very same subject might be very pleasant also.

Maybe next in line in popularity would be the species *Rosa*. The examples of roses in design, let alone in embroidery, are just too numerous to mention here. I find that I very often come back to roses in my work, not only in my botanical art work, but also in other ways of designing as well as in my embroidery. Being a born perfectionist (not always possible and therefore often frustrating) and having a great love for roses, I was driven to depict roses as accurately as possible.

This is how I was inspired to do almost every piece in this book: first, a love for a certain plant, and then the thought of what to make using a design incorporating the plant. Maybe for that reason, some plants have a somewhat chosen position in this book. Once I have selected a specific flower, the next step is to figure out a design.

I have based most of my designs in this book on one design or another, which I already have used for something else, such as magazine illustrations or fabric designs. I have also been inspired by favorite, long-admired art of the masters, photographs, magazines, and catalogs. In describing all the pieces in the following chapters, I will explain the derivations.

Once the basic design is arrived at, I decide how it can best be used. Then a choice of compatible fabric and thread or yarn is made. Not that this is always the necessary sequence of events. Often I am inspired by a fabric or a frame or a certain design to initiate a project, using one of my favorite flowers as the main subject.

As an example, in our bedroom we have a small and beautifully designed Empire chair. Apparently, it has had quite a history; if only it could talk! As with most chairs of that type, it has a loose seat. Further, this seat was in dire need of a new cover, so I decided to

* Paisley is the name of the place in Scotland where Paisley shawls originated. These were copies of Kashmir shawls.

petra

Die Monatszeitschrift für die Frau

Großer
Frühlings
Schönheits
Teil

4

petra erscheint
am letzten Mittwoch
jedes Monats.
Dies ist das
Aprilheft 1966.
Preis DM 1,50
Dänemark dkr 3,25
Italien Lire 300,—
Österreich S 10,—
Schweden skr 2,50
(inkl. oms)
Schweiz sfr 1,80
Spanien Ptas 40,—

embroider one. The cover on it was very old and must have been very pretty when it was new. It had tiny flowers in stripes alternating with satin-ribbon stripes. This all had faded through the years to a more or less all-over comfortable brown. Somehow, the chair's design reminded me of Malmaison and Napoleon's Josephine, and of her rose garden, and because of her rose garden, of Pierre Joseph Redouté, the painter *par excellence* of many of Josephine's roses.

Oddly enough, when I stripped the seat to be able to apply the new cover properly, I uncovered another somewhat older fabric of a similar nature. I couldn't help inspecting to see what was under that layer. To my surprise I found a very un-Josephine–Malmaison-like fabric that had once been a very Napoleonic jet black and multicolor striped grosgrain—or is it Ottoman?

Blues and roses came to mind as colors used much in the Empire period, and those were the colors I fixed on. Because the old fabric was striped, I decided the embroidery should be striped also. Seeing that there are no blue roses, the stripes would be blue, the roses rose and in garlands. No more complicated thought than that went into the project.

At this point I suppose I should reveal a secret long reserved to members of my immediate family: that I was born into a family of not only artistic, but also very pack-rat-like propensities. I must have started collecting fabrics and such at a very early age. As time passed, I found myself moving increasing amounts of fabrics from house to house, and after every trip to Europe my supplies grew, and my library was enriched. I will not, therefore, be able to recommend where to find many of the materials used in the book, because the source of some of them has escaped me. I will, however, list at the end (page 82) a few places where good fabrics can be found. I find that linens —fine, coarse, and in canvas form—are useful for most kinds of embroidery. Other fabrics, such as open-mesh canvas, bargello, upholstery fabrics, hopsacking, velvet, and others, all have their place in flower embroidery.

However, for cross-stitches to be even, it is really necessary to have even-weave material. Finding even-weave is quite difficult. There are, however, a few sources for such fabrics; the ones I know are also listed at the end. If you are lucky enough to be traveling to Europe,

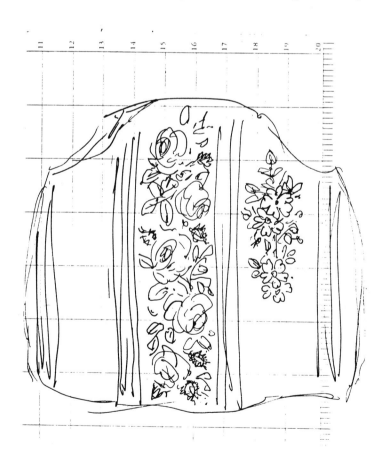

Original sketch for
rose seat cover

8

you'll find even-weave linens in many gauges and colors almost anywhere; a large amount of this material is supplied by Denmark and Switzerland.

Long ago I traveled to Denmark, where I found an embroiderer's heaven in the shop of Clara Waever in Copenhagen. It was a delight to buy all sorts of her designs; some came supplied with assorted D.M.C. thread in the designated colors and sufficient yardage of even-weave linen to get to work on the project any time. I bought so many such kits (the first of their kind, I think) that I figured it would take all the rest of my life to finish them. Just in case I should run out of kits, I bought some designs alone. These are charts representing the design printed on large sheets of graph paper and color coded. If you can read or translate Danish, the color codes are easy to figure out. Otherwise it takes quite a bit of brain-wracking to get the right results. It wasn't easy to find even-weave linen either. Instead of first finishing all the remaining kits, I set my mind on making one of the separate designs, a large mixed-flower wreath. It seemed logical to use it on a round linen tablecloth. No matter how hard I

Danish
tablecloth

9

searched, it was impossible to find even-weave at all, let alone any even-weave suitable for a round cloth. So I finally settled on a round Belgian-linen tablecloth. It wasn't even-weave, of course, but I thought it was practically so. As a result, I now have a slightly oval wreath on a round cloth! It really doesn't matter much, and probably people would never notice it, and if one is to make true cross-stitch work, the stitches should be square, and they can only be square with even-weave material. Then a round design will turn out round! In the chapter on cross-stitch I will show a way to use cross-stitches on uneven linen.

From a choice of fabric, the next step is to select suitable yarns and threads. I have always collected woolen yarns with the intention of some day using them for just the right project. I used to dye crewel wool just for the pure joy of concocting beautiful colors and as many shades as possible, especially floral colors and greens in large quantities. One can always use leftover colors for other projects, but when one needs a lot of one color (particularly unusual shades) and the project uses more than anticipated, it is extremely difficult if not impossible to match that color. Using many shades of one color, with very little variation on one project, is therefore one way to get around predicaments of this kind. Using more shades also enriches the basic color effect of the embroidery.

The colors of your yarns and threads are also most important, and, as I mentioned earlier, the best way to get colors you want and can't buy is to dye them yourself. Sometimes surprise colors develop that really are more suitable than what you had originally intended. When a commercially dyed yarn is not quite what you had in mind, try dyeing over the original color. It is just as simple, and some of the acquired new shades can be very rewarding. I try to match colors of yarn and thread with the actual colors of the flowers to be embroidered. But sometimes, to fit availability of colors, I make concessions, and as long as the results are harmonious and therefore pleasing and not too far removed from reality, I accept substitutes. I have always hated such things as kelly-green roses and brown leaves or purple lilies and blue leaves! The color combinations might be nice by themselves, but green roses and purple lilies are quite obnoxious to me. Any shade of red from near white to very dark burgundy-purple is very acceptable, even if not precisely correct for any rose type. Greens for leaves can be infinitely varied. I generally use two of three shades of warm green (for example, olive- or yellowish green) and two or three shades of cool green (for example, bluish or gray-green) for contrast in one piece of embroidery. Yellows and oranges are hard to find in floral shades, so here again dyeing to more subtle shades is appropriate.

When choosing the colors for the flowers, the background color should be kept in mind. The background and flowers can be in the same color range, but the shades should vary enough to give contrast. Light blue flowers on a dark blue background or dark blue flowers on a light blue background can be done, but dark on dark can be very disappointing.

Of course, dyeing woolen yarns is far more successful than dyeing cotton. Cotton can be dyed, but it really isn't worth the trouble; D.M.C. and other manufacturers produce so many shades of flower-like colors that a little searching will usually provide all the colors needed. Collect cotton thread—it's amazing how many different colors there are. One can even use more than one color at a time for extra richness, and so-called dyeing failures (irregularly dyed yarn) can even be used to advantage. I now like to "wallow" in colors—I use many. This may be the result of my childhood experience in grammar school in Holland. At that time third-grade girls were taught various needlecrafts, and I, having freshly arrived from America, had a new field of endeavor before me. The day came when I was to start my first real embroidery. It was cross-stitch (tiny) on even-weave linen with thread in a choice of colors: purple, lavender, dark orange, light orange, dark blue, light blue, and red. Nothing else!

Maybe that experience influenced me more than anything else to really use color generously, and, I might add, happily!

As for tools and equipment to make the pieces in this book, I would say in general—the usual. Anything that one feels one needs to add to one's skill and comfort in embroidering is acceptable. I use fine-pointed, very sharp embroidery scissors mostly. They are useful for many embroidery chores. Use eyeglass-hinge rings around a scissor joint to keep it tight. I often use a ripping prong. This item goes under several names, but whatever its name, it is very handy to cut and pick out mistakes and unwanted thread. I almost always use the same needle, a short, medium-sharp, large-eyed one, and I've worn out a few, believe it or not! Only when using such things as crewel

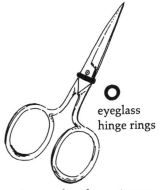

eyeglass hinge rings

sharp embroidery scissors

ripping prong

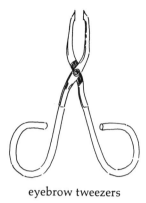

eyebrow tweezers

yarn on velvet have I used a thicker needle with a sharp point. In other words, when the background is a fine or tight weave, and the thread is coarse, use a heavier, sharper needle. The sharp point will enter the fabric easier, and will then spread the fibers wider to let the thread through without so much wear on either the fabric or the thread. One tool that I find very useful is an eyebrow tweezer of the kind with loops for the fingers. With very tricky pulling out of threads, etc., this comes in handy.

I think that the choice of hoops and frames to keep embroidery stretched while in progress is entirely up to the embroiderer. I use various kinds for various projects. These are the only ones I ever use. The advantage of using an unattached frame is that one can take it anywhere. One can almost always find a surface to support one end of the frame; this leaves both hands free to work entirely on the

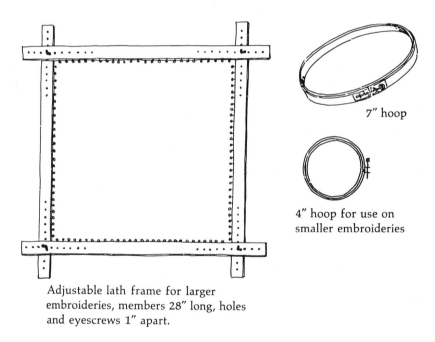

7" hoop

4" hoop for use on smaller embroideries

Adjustable lath frame for larger embroideries, members 28" long, holes and eyescrews 1" apart.

embroidery. To me this is comfortable, but I don't preclude the use of any other type of frame. The four-inch hoop turned out to be the handiest of all the stretchers; it is very easy to use, and moving it from one area of the embroidery to another doesn't present any difficulty.

Edging and finishing are very important, and sometimes they come before the embroidery proper. Edging and/or finishing fall into the whole concept of the design. Every piece of embroidery in this book was planned as a whole, finished product, never as just a piece of embroidery with no definite purpose. For instance, a certain picture frame will suggest a certain grouping of flowers, a chair's style will suggest a stripe, a pillow for a certain room will determine what type of material should be used, and, of course, if you think of a tablecloth or place mats, certain suitable materials and shapes will determine how the piece is to be worked.

In the case of "Haverhill Spring" or tulips and ixiolirion (page 33) I tried to accomplish an airy, light, springlike effect with a touch of "country." This seemed to lead to the lacy open-work edging, which would serve simultaneously as a frame with the wall-hanging effect, with the coarse burlap backing serving as a "country" touch. There are numerous booklets and books that will suggest any amount of open-work and plain edgings. I find the simple ones the most obvious and pleasing.

In this chapter I only roughly suggest how to approach flower embroidery. In the following chapters I will describe in detail how I went about doing each piece. I hope there will be other embroiderers who will be able to glean some ideas from what they find in this book.

Some examples of various types of edging

Flowers in Wool

Bouquet with Roses and Dutch Iris Picture
Wool embroidery on cotton upholstery broadcloth.

One summer day in New City, N.Y., where my mother lives, I saw a small bouquet my sister had picked, which was so appealing in its simple delicacy that I felt I should make either a drawing or a photograph of it for future reference. I have quite a stack of sketches and notes, which I hope some day to work into either paintings or embroideries. That day I just made a quick sketch and some notes, and only years later did I pick up the idea again to make an embroidery of it. I had the mustard-colored material on hand, and I had a good collection of suitable colors in crewel wool. The color of the background seemed to reflect the warmth of summer, and at the same time would be a good contrast to all the bouquet colors. In approaching the color choice of the yarn, I tried to stay as close as possible to the natural flower colors. This was long before I started this book, but even then I worked my embroidery as close to reality as possible. Crewel colors tend to be somewhat more subtle and subdued than true flower colors, but as long as all the different colors are of the same material, they seem to harmonize, and the difference, as compared to reality, really isn't very noticeable. Many of the more delicate colors I dyed myself, always with flower colors in mind. It is like mixing colors on a palette; in this case my palette is a large Mexican basket filled with wire clothes hangers, each with crewel yarn of one color and its shades all sorted.

First, the fabric was mounted on the embroidery frame after basting a very tight-weave linen strip around all the edges to prevent

Mexican basket with hangers of yarn.

raveling. The frame was adjusted to the proper size, and then with cotton buttonhole thread, the edges were sewn to the frame. I have never used upholsterer's string or thread, but I imagine it would be excellent for this use.

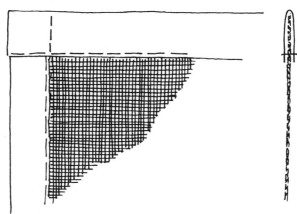

Binding and basting fabric with linen strips against raveling. Baste with back-stitch for strength.

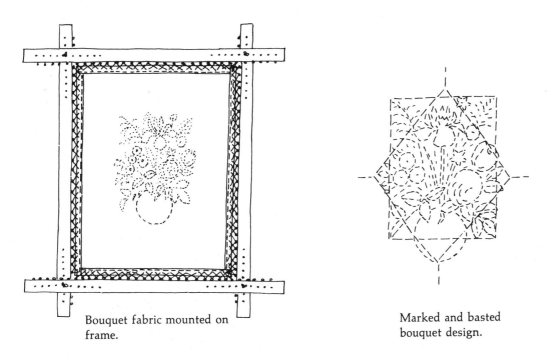

Bouquet fabric mounted on frame.

Marked and basted bouquet design.

Next, the precise center of the material was determined and marked with white basting thread. Here I should point out that the design was worked directly from the sketch to the fabric. I know my flowers well enough, and my sense of design is such that I think out where

Sketch on vellum

Transfer paper

Fabric

I will start putting each flower in the finished embroidery. However, it wouldn't be quite fair to my readers to just say "I did it." Better it would be to advise how it could be done.

A design could be sketched directly on such material as I have used here, with a light or white tailor's pencil. Ironing or steaming the finished sketch fixes it so that it won't rub off as easily while work progresses. If direct sketching is too difficult, another method can be used. In art stores one can acquire transfer paper (Saral in rolls or sheets) in colors: graphite, blue, red, yellow, and white. Depending upon the darkness of the color of the background, one of these should do well. The design should be traced through the paper onto the fabric. One drawback of this method is that the transferred design consists of an almost loose powder on the fabric, so basting of all the lines of the sketch will be necessary (roughly or in detail, depending upon how much guidance is needed) before starting the embroidery. The basting stitches pull out very easily as you progress with the work.

All of the stitches used in this piece are basically very simple ones, and need no further explanation. The finished picture was framed without glass.

16

5 Coral Bells
The coral-colored bells are made with lazy-daisy stitches, some with three tacks. The stems are whipped stem stitch and whipped running stitch.

6 Alchemilla
This flower is the most abbreviated in this bouquet. They are actually only random cross-stitches in two shades of yellow-green.

7 Rock pink
Magenta pink buttonhole stitch petals. Individual couching stitches in white (the crewel wool was split to get the tiny specks). The stamens are two straight stitches with a small French knot at the end of each. The stems are whipped stem stitch, and the leaves are buttonhole stitch.

8 Vase
Several shades of light-grey and white with grey-green accent in back-stitch at the bottom.

It should be noted that the more colors that are used in this kind of embroidery, the richer the end result will be.

Actual size: embroidery 6¾"x9", frame 9¼"x12".
Materials: gold-yellow hop-sacking, crewel wool.

1 Dutch Iris
Five shades of yellow and orange crewel wool worked in satin stitch. Stem and leaf light-green buttonhole stitch, one row overlapping the other.

2 Red centifolia rose
This was made by building up ridges of stem stitching; overcast and satin stitches were also used. Several shades of red were used. The leaves are made of back-stitch outlines and satin-stitch filler in shades of green.

3 Pink rose bud
Only satin stitch was used here in five shades of pink.

4 Multiflora roses
Each flower is made of white satin-stitch with yellow stamens, which are actually individual couching stitches. The centers are yellow-green satin-stitch with back-stitch accents. The stems are couched stem stitch with double lazy-daisy buds. The bud petals are buttonhole stitch in two shades of pink.

Daisy Quilt

Rectangular crazy-patch quilt with composite family flowers embroidered on the plain patches. All-wool-edge embroidery on all-wool or wool-blend fabrics (Viyella, etc.). The filling is a woolen blanket and the backing is Viyella with wool embroidery.

This piece was first conceived as a new way to make a quilt. It had nothing to do with flowers in particular, to begin with. I just love quilts, and it had been my intention to make a woolen one for quite some time; cotton quilts are all so heavy, and aren't very warm. So when I started collecting ideas for this book, I thought that by decorating the quilt with flowers, it would fit in. So I started the quilt first, and decided which flowers to use later.

I had been given a good Dutch blanket many years ago. It was still in fairly good shape but faded and worn smooth; it would serve very well as the filling. A length of Viyella I had stored away for some future use turned out to be just perfect for this purpose. The precise centers of the blanket and the backing were found, and these were basted together. The remainders of the Viyella were pieced together in such a fashion as to form a border with corner pieces. This was all

Two-color herringbone X –

Feather stitch O –

Chain stitch Z –

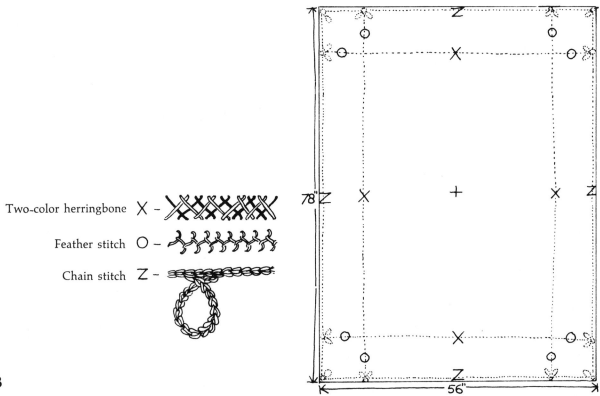

pinned and basted in place, and then embroidered. I used double herringbone stitch in two colors around the whole center section, chain stitch around the whole binding edge, and feather and chain stitches at the corners.

Then for the quilt itself. I had many swatches and leftovers of plain and printed woolen and part woolen cloth, and after some very kindly answered requests to my four sisters, who all sew their own clothing, I had more than enough material to complete the project.

I used crewel wool for all the edges. The stitches are too varied and numerous to list here. I would say the possibilities are infinite. No one edge is exactly the same as any other. It becomes quite fascinating to invent new edgings as the work goes along. Each patch is first pinned and then basted into place. The edging stitches not only connect the quilt pieces, but as they are made, they pick up a few fibers of the filling, which quilts the pieces at the same time. Each patch overlaps the previous one as you work toward the middle of the quilt.

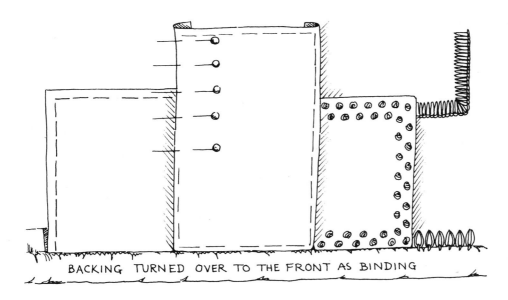

BACKING TURNED OVER TO THE FRONT AS BINDING

Time came to decide which flowers to use. Daisies seemed a good idea, and instead of just daisies, many kinds of daisylike flowers, such as asters, chrysanthemums, and black-eyed Susans. Coincidentally, I happened to see a picture in a *National Geographic* in which a farm woman from southwest Virginia displays her crazy quilt with, yes, daisies! (Oda Belle Blankenship, July 1972.) Done her way, but daisies! The daisy family was an excellent choice. There are plenty of species and varieties to be able to put a different one on each plain patch of the quilt with sunflower on the largest and center patch.

Embroidering these flowers was coming as close to stylizing as I did on any other piece in the book. They are all recognizable, though. I used all sorts of stitches, and my rule was generally very liberal here: use the stitches that seem most appropriate, and let the imagination go wild! Because of the nature of this embroidery, a sharppointed needle was used, but not too thin a one to facilitate pulling through the yarn.

Actual size: 56"x78"
Materials: All wool or combination wool fabrics, all crewel wool embroidery, woolen blanket padding.

1   Sunflower
The petals are all buttonhole stitch with satin-stitch filler in rows to simulate the "folds" of the real petals. Starting from the middle, the heart is made of spirally arranged brown stem-stitches with yellow satin-stitch filler. Small star-shaped disk florets are made of yellow back-stitches. Then a ¾" ring of brown and black loop stitches finishes the heart. Bits of dark-green calyx show at the base of the ray petals.

20

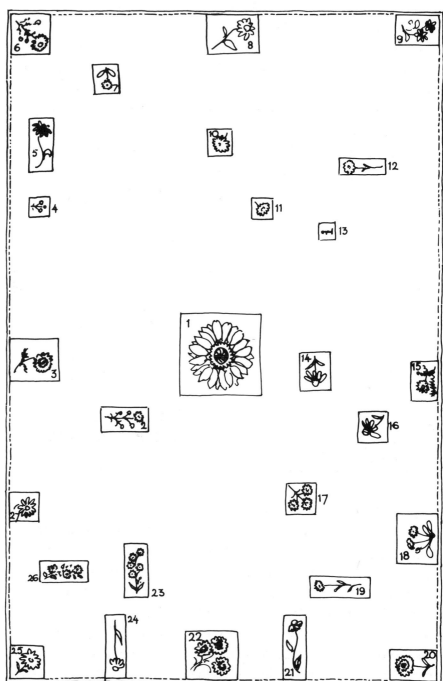

2 Pink chrysanthemum
The petals are lazy-daisy stitches, the center yellow loop stitches, and stems and leaves are made of stem-stitches and satin stitches.

3 Annual chrysanthemum
White, red, and yellow satin-stitches form the petals. Dark brown loop stitches and lighter brown satin-stitches form the center. The leaves are back-stitch, the stem is back-stitched chain stitch.

4 Wild aster
Tiny lazy-daisy stitches (thin white wool was used here) and tiny yellow French knots are all that is needed for this flower. The stem is back-stitch, the leaves lazy-daisy stitch.

5 Black-eyed susan
Deep yellow satin-stitch petals with darker yellow around the dark brown, very tightly packed turkey-stitch center. The center was clipped and shaped. The stem and leaves are whipped stem- and satin-stitch.

6 Pink chrysanthemum
Combination lazy-daisy stitches (one filling a larger one) were used for the petals. The center is made of two colors of yellow loop-stitches. The stems are two-tone whipped chain-stitch, the leaves open blanket-stitch.

7 Small English daisy
White straight stitches with pink lazy-daisy stitches on the outer edge to form the petals. The center is yellow loop stitch, very closely packed.

8 Gaillardia
Orange-yellow filled lazy-daisy stitches around red satin-stitch make the petals. The center is made of very dark brown loop stitches with light yellow stamens which are also loop stitches. The stem is whipped chain stitch, the leaves buttonhole stitch.

9 Senecio, dusty miller
Light yellow satin-stitch petals with darker yellow centers of turkey stitch are all that is needed for the flowers. The bud and stem are stem-stitch. The leaf is satin- and stem-stitch.

10 Chrysanthemum
A burnt orange color was used here in satin-stitch. The center is made of woven spider web-stitch.

11 Chrysanthemum
Purple-maroon is the only difference between this and the foregoing flower.

12 Small ox-eye daisy
The petals are satin-stitch, the center loop-stitch, the stem whipped stem-stitch, the leaves lazy-daisy stitch.

13 This square was used for my monogram.

14 Helenium
Red of a rather brownish hue in satin stitch was used for these petals. The center is a tight group of brown and light orange loop stitches with a "cap" of dark-brown satin-stitch.

15 Chamomile
Small white daisy-like flower made same way as #10 and #11. The leaves were done in back-stitch, and the stem is whipped chain-stitch.

16 Coneflower
The petals were satin-stitched in two shades of purple-red. The cone is made of dark maroon chain-stitch in very close rows to the top.

17 Fall aster
Straight-stitch petals in a deep wine red, make up these flowers. The centers are yellow loop stitch. The stems are stem-stitch, as are the leaflets.

18 English daisy
Small cherry-red lazy-daisy stitches and white and pink satin-stitch filler make the flowers. Yellow heart. The leaves are two shades of yellow green.

19 Fleabane
White straight-stitch petals, pink buds. Yellow turkey-stitch center. The stems are two-tone light green whipped stem-stitch, the leaves and bud filled stem-stitch.

20 Annual chrysanthemum
Yellow, orange, maroon circles of satin-stitch. The center is dark brown and maroon loop-stitch.

21 Yellow helenium
The petals are made of lazy-daisy and stem-stitches, and center red-brown loop-stitches and brown accent; the stem and leaves are stem- and buttonhole stitches.

22 Arctotis
Yellow, pink, and orange petals with dark centers of black and brown. The pink flower has circles of orange, pink, and yellow around the center. All petals are made of lazy-daisy and satin stitch. The stems and leaves are one shade of grey-green.

23 Aster
This wild Fall variety has small, white daisy-like flowers. They are made of radiating straight stitches with yellow turkey-stitch centers. The stems and leaves are light green stem- and buttonhole stitch.

24 Gazania
Dark yellow petals in satin-stitch with a center made of a ring of black lazy-daisy stitches with a white dot in each, and yellow turkey-stitch in the middle. The stems are green stem-stitch, the leaves dark-green satin-stitch.

25 Ox-eye daisy
This is made with straight-stitch and double-tacked lazy-daisy stitches. The center is made of yellow loop-stitch with a lighter yellow center of weave-stitch.

26 Sanvitalia
Yellow petals made of lazy-daisy stitches, the centers somewhat raised by packing yellow loop-stitches around very dark brown padded satin-stitch in the middle.

27 Alpine aster
Blue straight stitches form the petals. The center is made with yellow turkey-stitches around a small disc of pale-green weave stitch. The stem and leaf are stem-stitch.

Peony Pillow
Crewel embroidery on cotton upholstery velvet.

The peony pillow was directly derived from one of my illustrations for the then *Flower Grower Magazine*, for which I worked for many years as staff illustrator. That illustration was my own design, but in trying to think how I would suggest to others to find a design, I found that old Chinese silk paintings have not-dissimilar motifs. Such a design might be used as well. Also, other flowers could be used instead of peonies; suitable would be lilies, tulips, cyclamen, or tea roses.

Lilies

Tulips

Tea Roses

This piece was first mounted on the frame, which had been adjusted to fit the velvet. The velvet was edged with a firm-weave fabric before being laced to the frame with cotton buttonhole thread.

The transfer from my sketch to the velvet was done by first tracing the sketch on vellum (heavy) tracing paper, and then by placing a piece of transfer paper under the vellum face-down on the velvet and then following the design on the vellum with a small tracing wheel.

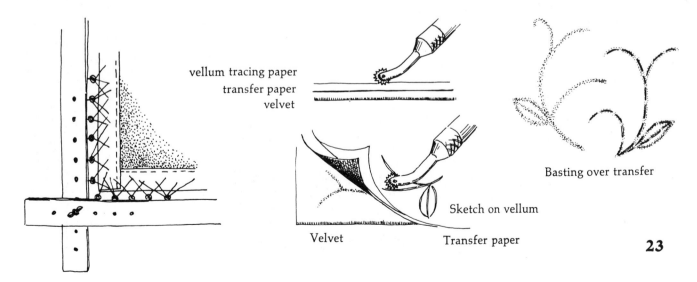

vellum tracing paper
transfer paper
velvet

Sketch on vellum

Basting over transfer

Velvet   Transfer paper

23

This process punches a minuscule amount of the transfer powder from the paper into the pile of the velvet. Here again it is best to baste all the lines before embroidering because the powder tends to brush off very easily.

The thread used for this embroidery was all Persian yarn; although regular crewel would be just as suitable, I preferred the silky sheen the Persian yarn possesses. Most of the colors were commercially available, but I added some, mostly greens, which I had dyed myself. In this case some of the greens would have been considered mistakes or improperly dyed. I found that the threads that were part of the "spots" in the skeins gave the leaves a richness of color acquired in no other way.

Actual size: pillow 15"x18", embroidery 12½"x15".
Materials: green upholsterer's velvet, all crewel wool,
 mostly Persian type.

1   Each petal in this flower was first outlined with
buttonhole stitch. Satin stitch was used as a filler
throughout. Four shades of dark red.

2   This peony was worked in the same fashion as #1;
the stamens are many whipped stem stitches in four
shades of yellow and orange. The brilliant pink pistils
are lazy-daisy stitches.

3   Five graded shades of pink were used, worked in
the same way as the first two flowers. Again the center
is made as in #2.

4   The outer petals have three shades of dark pink;
the center ones have five. The embroidery is the same
as in the other flowers.

5   This flower again is worked as the others are. Six
shades of yellow were used.

6   Five shades of light pink were used for this flower;
the same stitches.

The stems are all several rows of stem-stitch. Leaves
are all done in the same way as the flowers—buttonhole
stitch outlines and satin-stitch filler, stem-stitch veins.
It should be noted that the stitches always follow the
shapes of petals and leaves, and consequently one can
indicate the shapes of the petals and leaves by steering
the stitches in a certain direction. It can be quite
surprising and satisfying to see what the untraditional
use of a stitch can do. Small ruffles in a petal or a wave
in a leaf can be achieved by using the same basic stitch,
in this case buttonhole stitch, the same thread, in this
case crewel wool, but different tension or length of each
stitch. Nothing gives embroidery a mechanical and
monotonous appearance so much as stitches with
regular spacing.

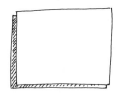

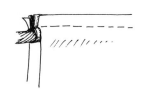

Step 1 Make piping long enough to go around entire pillow.

Step 2 Cut back piece same size as front.

Step 3 Wrong sides out, baste and seam with piping between layers. Leave part of seam open for stuffing.

Step 4 Turn inside out and stuff. Sew open seam overhand.

Double blanket-stitch edging.

Spring Flowers Trim for Collar and Cuffs
All cashmere and mohair kid yarn embroidery on cashmere fabrics.

There is a painting by Botticelli called *Primavera* (Spring). Primavera herself is clad in a lovely flowing garment with various spring flowers in small vignettelike clusters scattered over it. Schiaparelli, the famous silk manufacturer, has a showroom in Rome on the Via Sistina. When, once upon a time, I happened to pass the showroom, I noticed a copy of that same Botticelli dress. It consisted of silk embroidery (probably woven in, but it appeared to be embroidered) on heavy shell-colored silk satin. It was something so beautiful that I couldn't take my eyes off it. I just stood there admiring it, dreaming that maybe some day I would do the same kind of copying for my own use. I used to dream a lot about such things, but through the years I have come down to earth considerably, and doing more practical things occupies me quite enough. Then, long afterward, one of the mailing pieces of a book publisher had a reproduction of Primavera's head on the outside of the envelope. She had small spring flowers in her hair and a garland of the same flowers around her neck. This effect is actually what set off a sequence of sketches getting simpler and simpler as I continued with the thought of embroidering something that would reflect Primavera. The final version, far removed from the original, is this idea for trimming. This same trim could be used on dresses, sweaters, blouses, pillows, and if embroidered in cotton, as an edging for place mats or tablecloths.

26

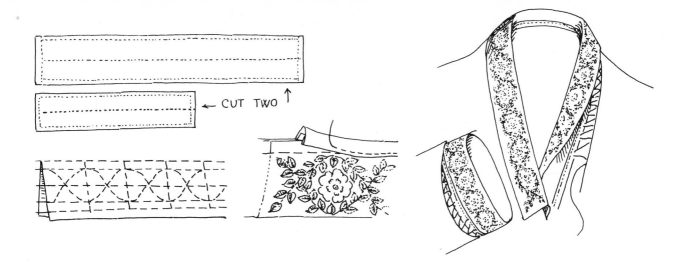

The strips were cut first to fit collar-and-cuff pattern pieces. Enough margin should be allowed on one side when folded to provide space for finishing when the embroidery is finished. All pieces are lined with thin, firm cotton, cut on the bias. In my example the white cashmere fabric was cut (unabashedly) from a tired cashmere sweater, and several colors of cashmere and Ayrshire-kid-mohair (no longer commercially available) yarns were used for the embroidery. Any jersey fabric and fingering yarn would do as well.

The folding line, the center, the edges, and the rough design are basted as shown. The twisting branches are embroidered first, then the leaves. The resulting rounds are filled with one flower each. All the stitches are simple, as usual. I worked through all three layers of fabric, which gave a nice, firm finished product. No frame or hoop was used for this. The cut edge was finished with bias tape, and tacked to the inside of the garment.

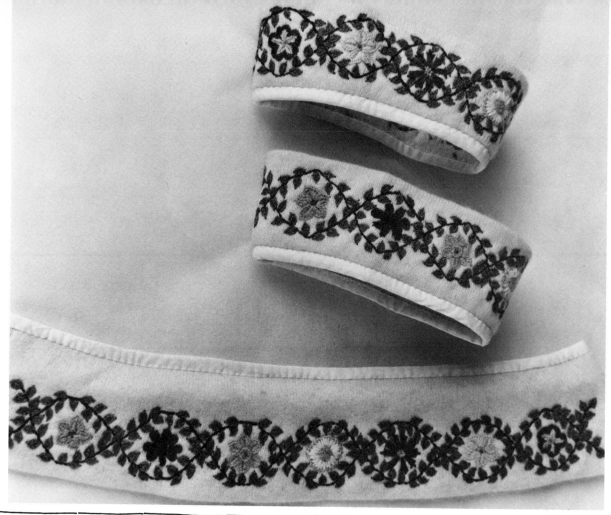

Actual size: embroidery 2"x13½".
Materials: cream-white cashmere; cashmere and kid
   mohair yarn.

1 Primrose
The petal outlines are buttonhole stitch (red). The
center is a combination of pale yellow fishbone stitch,
close overcast stitch in dark yellow, and a single green
French knot.

2 Jasmine
The stitches used for this pale-yellow flower's petals
are really only one stitch, buttonhole, but used as
herringbone. The center is dark-yellow overcast with a
single green French knot.

3 Cornflower
The petals are elongated double lazy-daisy stitches with
three tacks to a petal.

4 Bellis Daisy
Each petal is a single straight stitch in white with a
"cap" of two small pink back-stitches. The center is
made up of close loop stitches (yellow).

5 Jonquil
The petals are made as in #2. The center is buttonhole
stitch around a central point with a tiny green French
knot in the middle of it. The flower is yellow.

6 Anemone
The petals are a combination of buttonhole stitch
around a central point with a tiny green French knot in
the middle of it. The flower is yellow.

7 Bluebell
Lavender-blue petals in the same way as #2 and #5.
The center is made with three green back-stitches.

All of the leaves are buttonhole stitch in the same
grey-green, the stems dark green back-stitch.

Primrose Basket

All crewel wool on bargello canvas, making use of bargello and varied crewel stitches.

My memories of my grandmother are many, but one stands out in particular. She used to carry a small black satin bag around with her wherever she went, in or out of the house. In it were all sorts of things that she wished to have at hand at all times: keys, handkerchief, eau de cologne, pills, etc. I always thought that a very practical idea. Of course, such a bag was small, and for my needs, at least, not anywhere near large enough. I need something to keep my current embroidery in so I can take it with me from room to room, and for this a decorative satchel is quite attractive. Why primroses? Well, I just like them particularly! And why a basket? I really don't know where that idea came from!

No frame or hoop was used for this embroidery. I think the canvas gives enough resistance to the tugs and pulls of normal embroidery. All the yarn for the flowers is crewel wool. The basket-weave bargello is all Persian yarn. There is only a very subtle difference in the appearance of the yarns, but I felt it would strengthen the contrast of the flowers against the basket. The finishing off is done by joining the pieces together, first basting and then double buttonhole stitching.

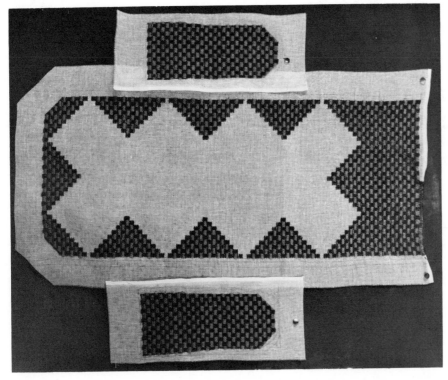

Pieces of
Primrose Basket
(main and side pieces
embroidered with
basket-stitch bargello)

Actual size: 10½"x25".

Materials: bargello canvas, crewel wool, mostly Persian-type; background two shades of straw color, Persian-type crewel wool.

All the flowers and leaves are done in the same way, buttonhole stitch outlines with satin stitch filler. The leaves have built-up edges here and there to achieve a three-dimensional effect. The 'build-up' is accomplished by embroidering buttonhole stitch rows, row upon row, disconnected from the canvas. The background should be continued under the build-up so that no bare canvas shows. The centers of the flowers are all the same: satin-stitch in light yellow with accents of orange in straight stitch. A light-green French knot circled by dark-green back-stitches, finishes the center. The stems are whipped stem-stitch in light green. The buds are buttonhole stitch. The background stitch behind the leaves is dark green, darning weave. Four greens were used for the leaves. The background for the whole embroidery is a two-tone tan bargello in basket-weave pattern (six threads light up and down, six threads dark back and forth).

Primrose 1
White outline, pale yellow filler.
Primrose 2
Outline bright orange, lighter orange filler.
Primrose 3
Dark magenta outline, magenta filler.
Primrose 4
Burnt orange outline, orange filler.
Primrose 5
Outline straw yellow, filler lighter straw yellow.
Primrose 6
Purple outline, filler a slightly bluer and lighter purple.
Primrose 7
Yellow outline, yellow filler.
Primrose 8
Outline red, filler orange.
Primrose 9
Deep blue outline, lighter blue filler.
Primrose 10
Cool dark-red outline, cherry red filler.
Primrose 11
Outline primrose yellow, filler light yellow.

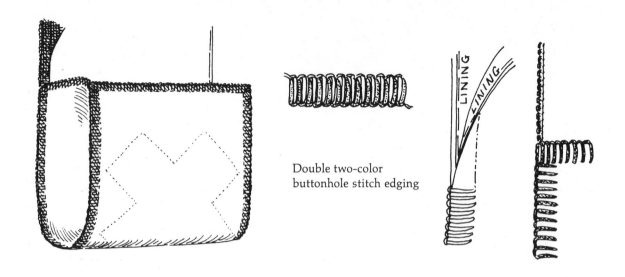

Double two-color
buttonhole stitch edging

The Primrose Basket completed

Flowers in Cotton

"Haverhill Spring." Tulips, Ixiolirion, and Others, Wall-hanging Picture

All D.M.C. six-strand cotton thread on napkin linen, mounted on and backed by dark-blue burlap.

This idea came from my garden in Haverhill, New Hampshire. My husband and I came up from New York some years ago to live in this lovely old town. We bought an 1810 brick house with a few acres of land. Parts of the land had been long used as garden, some with open light, and some tree-shaded and damp. In the damp part, someone long ago (I'm told at least twenty years) planted tulips in two long, straight rows. Through the years these tulips naturalized, and although the rows can still be discerned, the tulips have spread over quite a large part of what my husband named the "farouche garden." Realizing that the tulips are really unusual and precious, I tried not to disturb them, and I am now trying to cultivate a studied casual garden that will live up to the interesting name my husband gave it. Those tulips have taken a very special place in my heart. There are several hundreds of them, mostly the same pinky red variety (I haven't found its proper name so far). A few other varieties take their place there, but they are few in number, and therefore not very noticeable. The ixiolirions and all the other species in this design are growing in "the farouche." I planted them there, but they haven't

33

spread far as yet. They are promising, however. Of these flowers the ixiolirions, in particular, seem to like Haverhill, and it being one of my favorite bulb flowers, I gave it prominence in this piece.

The round design is based on an illustration I did for *Flower Grower* many years ago. That design was of only white flowers and green foliage to accommodate the two-color printing for which it was intended. When I first thought of this design as an embroidery, I was going to use only white and green thread, which might have been pretty. However, there being no limitations as to color here, I settled on using as much color as possible.

A Japanese linen napkin with artificially hand-hemmed edges was to be the background of this piece. The material was rather open-woven and light; this was fine for the airiness I was looking for, but for the type of embroidery I was going to use, it needed some support. I used white tie-facing material, which would later be snipped away as close as possible around all the flowers from the back of the work.

The edges were cut off the napkin, and the remaining material trimmed to be square and even all around. The edging to serve as frame was embroidered first. Then the precise center was found, and with the tie-facing in place, basted. After that, the circle, which would be the outline of the design, was basted in. Then a second circle was basted ¼″ around the first. The outer circle actually indicates the limit of how far one can extend the flowers and leaves from the inner circle without distorting the round design.

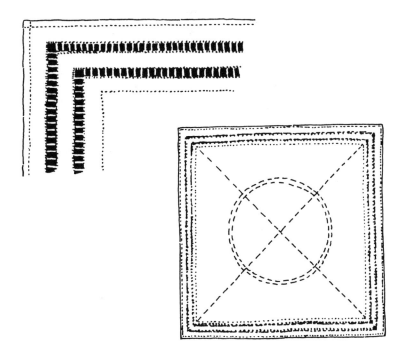

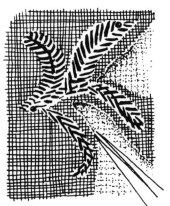

Use extreme caution not to cut through front.

When the embroidery is finished, trim away the superfluous tie-facing from the back of the embroidery. Then the embroidery should be washed and ironed after being towel-dried, but while still damp. In this case this step should be taken now, because once the embroidery has been attached to the burlap backing, it can't be washed any more. In time, when necessary, the embroidery will have to be removed from the burlap to be cleaned.

35

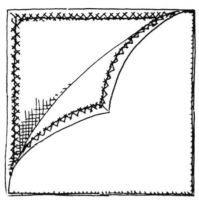

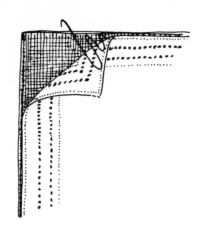

Turn all burlap edges under
and overcast to inside. Then
sew front to back seams
inside.

Tack linen to burlap.

Cut a square of burlap that will fit around the linen embroidery with a ¼″ margin when turned under and hemmed. Another piece of burlap of the same size should be turned under and back-stitched to the first piece. When this is finished the embroidery is tacked to the burlap.

Cut a length of ¼″ dowel to fit, just a little short at each end, the top side of the hanging. Attach this dowel to the back of the burlap with firm stitches about ½″ from the top edge. Hang by the dowel.

I used a large hand-hoop frame for this, shifting it to the necessary location as the work proceeded.

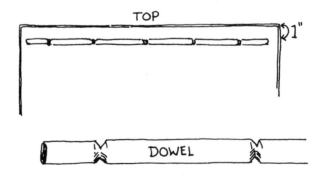

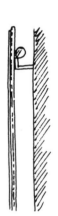

TOP

1″

DOWEL

Carve notches in dowel at 1″ from both ends and
in center, also half way between center and end
on both sides. The notches will hold the stitches
so they can't slip.

38

Actual size: 8″ diameter, whole finished embroidery 16″x16″.

Materials: white loose-weave linen, two strands D. M. C. six-strand cotton used throughout.

All the flowers and leaves are done in my favorite stitches, buttonhole and satin. A few accents and details are done in other stitches, and they are mentioned in the individual descriptions below.

1 'Broken' tulip
Two shades red and white, and two shades off-white for shadows. Base yellow-green, all satin stitch.

2 Pink tulips
Three shades of pink-red; base is white, light-blue, and dark-blue. All satin stitch except a buttonhole accent along petal edge.

3 Pheasant-eye narcissus
The eye itself is a circle of red buttonhole stitch; narrow rows of yellow, orange, and green satin stitch, three yellow-green French knots.

4 Tulip leaves
Five shades of light-green, all satin stitch.

5 Bleeding heart
Two shades of pink were used for "hearts". Three shades of pale pink for the "drops."

6 Canadian phlox
Pale blue grading to white around the center which is dark blue. The buds darker blue than the petals.

7 Woodruff
Each floret is made of four white lazy-daisy stitches with light-green stamens.

8 Yellow primrose
Petals have three shades of yellow, and the centers three. A light-green French knot in the middle.

9 Triandrus narcissus
Three shades of white form the petals, the cup two shades of cool yellow, the leaves dark blue-green.

10 Forget-me-not
Blue petals, pink bud petals. The center is made with white back-stitches between petals, and a yellow thread passed through the white stitches.

11 Lily of the valley
White and two shades light yellow-green used in padded lazy-daisy stitches.

12 Ixiolirion
Four shades of blue used in satin stitch only, centers navy blue and grey accent stitches.

13 Johnnie-jump-ups
The two upper petals are purple, the middle two petals are white with bits of yellow, the lower petal two shades of yellow and black. The center accent is white.

14 Jonquil
Bright jonquil yellow with light yellow-green accents and tiny French knot in center.

15 Periwinkle
The blue this flower gave its name to is hard to find, but worth looking for. The center is white with a green French knot.

Carnation Tablecloth

D.M.C. six-strand cotton worked on commercial linen tablecloth. The fringe was made of same tablecloth.

There really was no preconceived design for this piece. I had the tablecloth first, and the idea for the design gradually developed. The fringe was the first part of the development. I had made fringes on earlier embroideries. They are fun to do, and make a very effective finishing for tablecloths. The machine-stitched edges at each end were undone (the other two edges are selvages) and then the material was cut into strips about 1″ wide toward the center of the cloth, following the threads carefully so as not to cut into them midway. Then all the resulting short pieces of cross-threads (woof thread) were pulled out. There now were the long threads to knot together in small bunches to make the fringe.

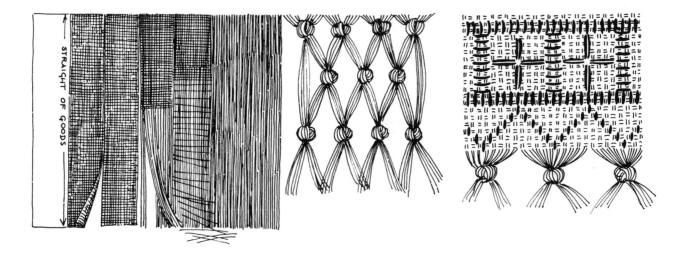

I then made an edging of drawn-fabric work to fit the fringe. The squares aren't absolutely necessary, but I liked the effect. Any other such stitchery could be used as well. I next divided and marked the remaining (unembroidered) material so that I would have a kind of plaid effect. Then the single faggot stitches were embroidered. The lines were started at one end and worked all the way through to the other end, following a thread. The stitches were pulled tight so that small holes appeared. (The spaces between the resulting squares will vary according to the measurements of the cloth.) I found this took quite a bit of figuring, calculating, and pinning and marking. However, once the right measurements are found, the whole pattern materializes easily when the lines are embroidered. I chose to place flowers in the squares only; this gives a rather geometric but open design. Other possibilities are legion. Again, a large hoop was used for this work. The flowers had no particular set design; they were sketched in each square directly with tailor's pencil.

The finished tablecloth can be washed in cool water with real soap, and preferably by hand.

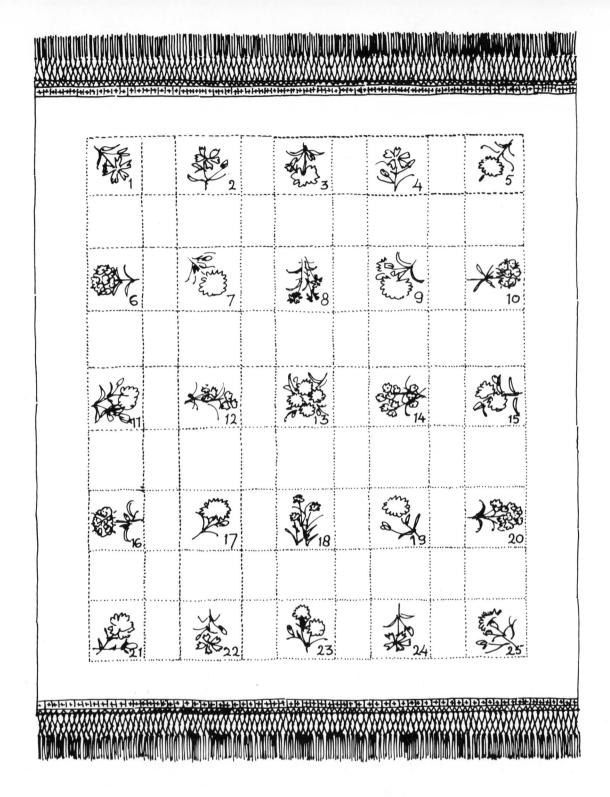

Actual size: 65" (with fringe) x52", flower squares 5¾".
Materials: two-tone red linen, all three-strand D. M. C.
six-strand cotton.

1 White, single-fringed annual pink.
2 Single garden pink, two shades of pink.
3 Light-orange border carnation.
4 Single annual pink, white and red.
5 Border carnation, yellow.
6 Sweet william, dark-red and black.
7 Border carnation, light red.
8 Small bright red rock pink.
9 Large pink nursery carnation.
10 Sweet william, red and white.
11 Salmon border pink.
12 "Knappi", yellow rock pink.
13 "Lacy lass", laced pinks, semi-double.

42

14 Wild "Deptford" pink, magenta.
15 Pink bunch carnation.
16 Sweet william, pink calico.
17 Orange double nursery carnation.
18 White and red rock pink.
19 Bright pink Chabaud carnation.
20 Sweet william, red.
21 Yellow and red striped "bizarre" carnation.

22 Single perennial pink, two shades of pink.
23 Red bunch carnation.
24 Single annual "China" pink.
25 Salmon pink Chabaud carnation.

All the flowers and leaves are done in the same fashion. Only occasionally were other stitches used for accents. The green of all of the leaves is grey-green—there are many shades of grey-green.

Forget-me-not and Pansy Place Mats
D.M.C. six-strand cotton embroidery on hopsacking.

The forget-me-nots are very similar to a design I keep coming back to. I used it in *Flower Grower* once, later as a textile design, and now here it is as an embroidery. As I mentioned in the first chapter, the background color can contribute to the general richness of color if it offers enough of a contrast to the embroidery, be it light or dark. The blue hopsacking was enough darker than the forget-me-nots to provide sufficient contrast and still remain in the same color range.

In the pansy place mat I used the reverse contrast. Darker yellows and greens on a pale yellow background. The design is once again an old one.

Both place mats were handled in the same way. The finishing edges were first worked around the edges. The forget-me-not place mat has an extra single faggot stitch line and sectioning.

The same stitches were used for the flowers. These two items were both made with the use of a small hand hoop. It wasn't necessary, but it made a flatter and neater kind of embroidery. Both can be washed very well as long as cool water and real soap are used. Hand washing is recommended.

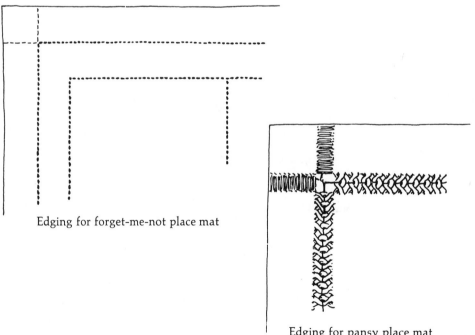

Edging for forget-me-not place mat

Edging for pansy place mat

44

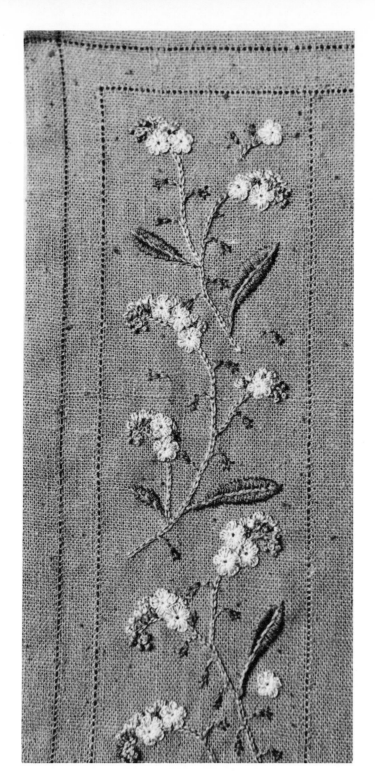

Forget-me-nots

Actual size: place mat 12"x17½"; flower panels
 10"x2½".

Materials: deep blue muslin, two strands D. M. C. six
 strand cotton.

The flower petals are made of four buttonhole stitches
each. The color, of course, is forget-me-not blue! The
center of each flower is made by drawing the thread
(two strands of white D. M. C.) through the same hole
and back-stitching between the petals (5x) pulling the

thread tightly so that an "eye" results. Finish by
threading two strands of yellow D. M. C. through
white stitches.

The stems are light-green chain-stitch. The closed buds
are tiny French knots. The open buds are made with
lazy-daisy (detached chain-stitch tacked down three
times) stitches (light green) and the bud petals are pink
buttonhole stitch. The seed pods are the same lazy-
daisy stitches with three tacks, using a darker green.
The same green is used for the leaves which are done in
satin stitch, the center in light green stem stitch.

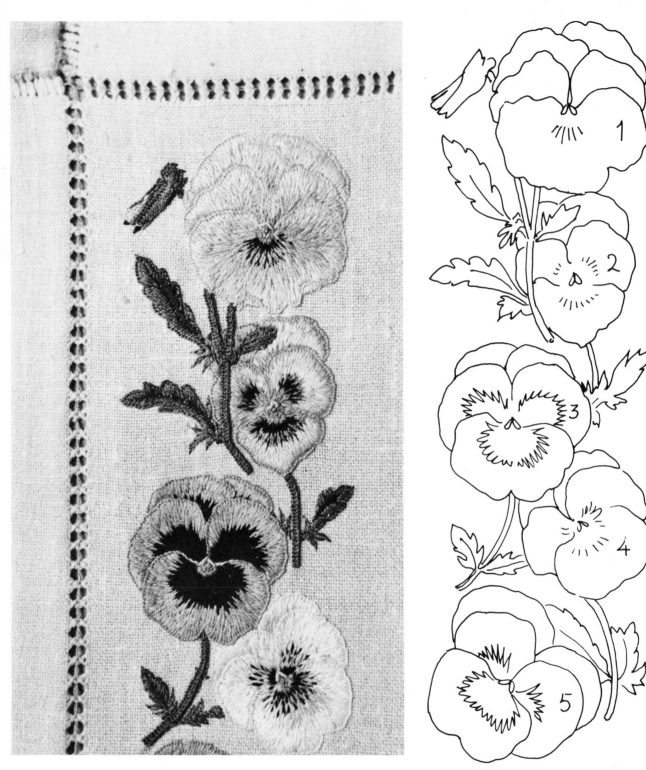

Pansies

Actual size: place mat 12"x16½", embroidery 9"x2¾".
Materials: pale yellow dress linen, two strands D. M. C.
   six-strand cotton.

In essence all five pansies are worked in the same way: buttonhole stitch outlines and satin-stitch filler. The variations are in the basic shapes and the colors. All the centers are the same: two white bullion stitches, a very small light green French knot in between, and a few tiny orange-red accent stitches (sometimes scarcely visible).

The leaves are also buttonhole-stitch outlined with satin-stitch filler (three shades of green). The stems, which in reality are square, can be made by making two facing and joining rows of buttonhole stitches with a row of stem-stitch over the middle. This gives the illusion of square stems.

These two designs could be used for other items such as trim on cuffs and collars of linen dresses or blouses, and pillows.

Pincushion

(Johnnie-jump-ups, rock pinks, alchemilla, and ageratum—viola tri-color, dianthus, alchemilla glabra, and ageratum.) D.M.C. six-strand cotton on green Irish dress linen.

This small pincushion may be the easiest item in the book. All the pieces were cut from remnants of dress linen. There should be enough to make four rounds for the top and bottom, a double strip for the side, and a long strip for the ruffle. Cut a perfect circle of paper, using a compass. Use this as a pattern for the top and bottom pieces. Mark the center of the two top pieces, and baste another circle around it. Now make your design to fit the circle. Transfer with transfer paper, and embroider. The stitches once more are very simple.

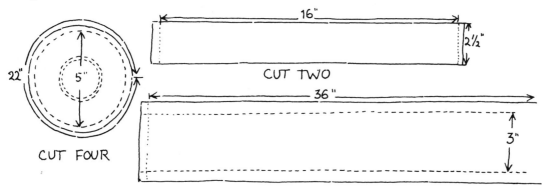

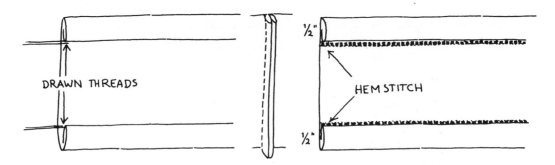

DRAWN THREADS

HEM STITCH

½"

½"

The ruffle strip is hemstitched on both sides, and the ends are seamed together. If you are going to wash the finished top, now is the time to do it.

To finish the pincushion you'll need a round of hard cardboard of the same size as the top and bottom (without a seam allowance). This cardboard will give a flat bottom to the pincushion. The cardboard is inserted into the partially seamed pincushion before stuffing. The stuffing I used was a bag full of woolen yarn ends and clippings. (I keep everything, and I always knew these would come in handy sometime!) Other stuffings are just as suitable as long as the pincushion is stuffed tightly. The unsewn part of the bottom seam is stitched overhand. The gathered ruffle is then tacked to the bottom seam.

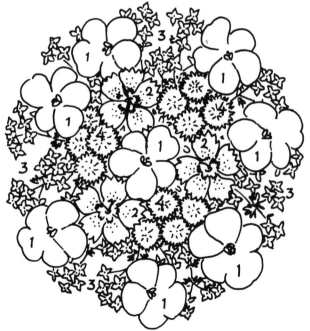

Actual size: 3" diameter, top of pincushion 5½".
Materials: green dress linen, two strands D. M. C. six-
  strand cotton.

1 Johnnie-jump-ups
Two upper petals are purple, three lower petals are
made with five shades of blue and purple. The "eyes"
are made of tiny French knots in red, green, and white
with yellow accents.

2 Rock pinks
Rock-pink red is a special red, close to magenta. White
specks and throat and black stamens and petal
markings finish these simple little flowers.

3 Alchemilla
Each floret is made of four lazy-daisy stitches, the color
a kind of yellow-chartreuse. The stems and leaves are
slightly greener, and made of straight- and back-
stitches.

4 Ageratum
The best description of the stitch used here is padded
satin-stitch, each thread, however, placed in a radial
direction rather than parallel as in true satin-stitch.
Two blues were used.

Empire Stripe Chair Seat

(rosa centifolia muscosa and rosa multiflora). D.M.C. six-strand cotton embroidery on crash linen.

Precise measuring and stretching are essential for this seat cover. It doesn't pay to try to get away with inaccuracies, as I admit I often do where possible. As with so many old chairs, the measurements are not exactly symmetrical. The only way to be accurate, it seemed to me after quite a bit of tape-measuring and sketching, was to take the to-be-used material and to stretch and pin it over the existing seat. With a tailor's pencil I drew lines between the pins. Then I determined the center, and marked it with basting thread. I also determined where the cover would be tucked in by the uprights of the chair back, and marked parallel lines at equal distances from the center from the uprights to the front of the seat. The three resulting lines are the guidelines for the rose garlands.

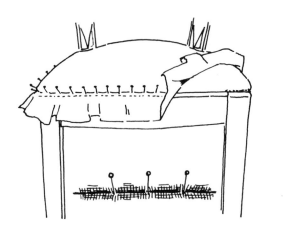 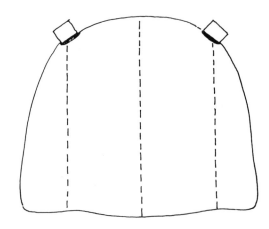

I then made my design to fit the outlines of the cover. As I explained earlier, the roses were decided on because to me they were reminiscent of the Empire period, particularly of Josephine Bonaparte and Redouté. Both moss roses and multiflora roses were in vogue at that time. The blue stripes with lacelike edges were a bit of fancy, a little frivolous, maybe, but in the end pleasing, I think.

The flower design was next worked out and transferred to the linen with the help of transfer paper. Before transferring the design, the linen was mounted on canvas, and then stretched on the frame

50

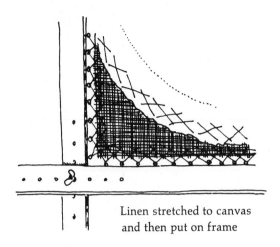

Linen stretched to canvas
and then put on frame

The design indicated
by basting stitches

with buttonhole thread. The design was next basted in. A helpful
hint here would be to suggest using basting thread in the colors of
flowers and leaves. If the basting is done in small stitches, pulling
it out on completion of the work will be unnecessary. Also, with
small stitches the basting will be more accurate. The multiflora garlands are more or less symmetrical, and were handled in the same
way as the moss roses.

A neat edging around the showing edge gave the finishing touch.
The finished embroidery was washed and ironed with real soap and
cool water and a not-too-hot iron—on the back of the material, of
course. The cover was then once again stretched and pinned over
the seat. To secure the embroidery, a backing was used rather than
tacks, which had been used previously several times so that the wood
had become fairly fragile.

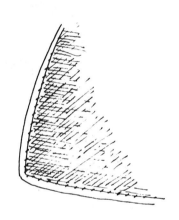

Backing of seat
instead of tacks

Stripe is 2" wide. Center is made of
white double flannel stitch tacked
in the middle. Each resulting square
is filled with a dark pink French
knot and the triangles with tiny
dark red cross-stitches. The
bargello stripes are four graded
shades of blue. Next comes a dark
green chain stitch, then a row of
buttonhole stitch in grey-green,
then another chain stitch in very
pale green, another grey-green
buttonhole stitch row reversed.
The outside row consists of beige
flannel stitch and French knots.

51

Actual size: 15"x16", stripes 2" wide.
Materials: natural-color crash linen, two strands
  D. M. C. six-strand cotton except the blue bargello
  stripes which were done with four strands.

All of the roses and leaves are done in the stitches I use
most: buttonhole stitch for outlines and satin stitch as
filler, back-stitch, stem-stitch, and French knots are the
only other stitches used in the garlands. The mossy
effect of the buds is made with multiple back-stitches
of varied size.

Cross-stitch
in Wool or Cotton

Cross-stitch is perhaps the most popular embroidery stitch ever. Maybe it is because its effective simplicity cannot be improved upon. Not only does the history of the cross-stitch go way back, but people in countries too far removed from each other in ancient times to know anything about each other made cross-stitches in their embroidery as if they had been taught to do so by one teacher. Where this fits into evolution I dare not speculate; to me such things are the wonders of the world.

In this chapter I will attempt to show just a few of the infinite uses of the stitch. Because of its geometric nature, cross-stitch tends to oversimplify flowers, but in spite of that, it really is surprising how many details one can achieve with just a few stitches. With the help of good colors, almost any flower can be made identifiable. I feel that my use of back-stitch in combination with cross-stitch is quite acceptable because it is used only to accentuate otherwise rather unclear shapes.

Using regular cross-stitch in any size is very easy. If one has a design to work from, it is only necessary to have the materials to to work with and a fair amount of patience to count out threads, and most of the patience is needed at the start of the work. Once the guidelines have been established, it is just a case of finding the corresponding place on the design from where to begin embroidering.

To make your own design, start with a pencil sketch of the general idea. Transfer this sketch to graph paper, and define the outlines a

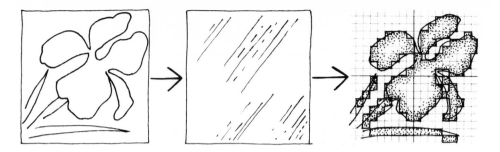

bit more clearly. Now with colored pencil, ball-point, or felt-tip pens, fill in each graph square (equal to one stitch) with the colors later to be translated into thread. Every line of leaves and flowers will have to be broken up into straights and squares as opposed to curves and rounds. It is quite a challenge to achieve the effect of a round petal or a toothed leaf, but the process is fascinating, and it's remarkable how close one can come to the true shape. One great advantage of using this method is that once your design has been worked out in squares and in color, you can see what your embroidery will look like when finished.

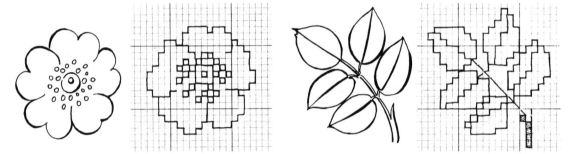

Another method of transfer, which can best be used for such things as pillows or pictures when canvas is used, and which I used for the second piece in this chapter, is as follows. The design is first sketched lightly, directly on the canvas, and then colored in so that the general design is clearly defined. The threads of the canvas will indicate where the threads will and will not be used. Where the sketch crosses the threads unevenly or only partly, no stitch will be made. This method takes still less effort than the first method. No threads to count!

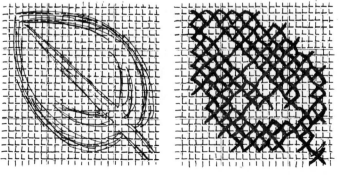

Crewel Bouquet, see page 14

Spring Flowers, see page 33

Field Flowers, see page 55

African Violets, see page 76

Ring of Roses,
see page 58

Carnation Tablecloth,
see page 40

Bulb Flowers Tablecloth, see page 63

Collar and Cuffs, see page 26

Chair Seat, see page 50

Primrose Basket, see page 29

Rose Place Mat,
see page 70

Pansy Place Mat, see page 46

Forget-me-not Place Mat, see page 44

Fall Bouquet, see page 72

Haverhill Field Flowers Picture

Mixed cross-stitches and back-stitches. Mixed cotton threads on white upholstery linen.

Behind our house we have a rather large open field, which bursts into bloom each summer. The flowers used for this piece are the kinds to be found in this field. They usually grow in patches, but here and there the plants intermingle, and the flowers twist and twine together not too unlike the effect of my bouquet design.

The material used is fairly heavy, pure white upholstery linen. I used both Danish flower thread (broder) and D.M.C. six-strand. The threads were used both singly and in multiples to give added variation to the stitches. The colors match only in the same flowers. For each species a separate group of colors was chosen. This also was done for variation, and gives a more lively effect. The needle was again a short, medium dull-pointed, large-eyed one, for no other reason than that I prefer working with this kind.

The sketch for the design was traced onto the linen with the help of transfer paper, and then retraced with a tailor's pencil, and after that ironed so the lines would set somewhat.

The stitches vary individually in size, in shape, and in grouping. In some cases I used tiny cross-stitches in lines or in an irregular filler way. In another case large irregular stitches were used in a regular fashion, as in the clover. Anything that seemed appropriate at the point when I started each specific flower was used. No rules of up and down or across! This use of cross-stitch (and back-stitch) is the most inspiring, but not the easiest.

Actual size: 10"x8⅝".
Materials: white upholstery linen, Danish "broder" thread, D. M. C. six-strand cotton.

1 Hawkweed
Random small cross-stitches roughly in up-and-down rows in five graduated colors (burnt orange to yellow). Centers red-brown broder thread, stems are overlapping cross-stitches with horizontal back-stitches used for hairy effect (green). Buds are cross-stitches with back-stitch hairs (green and brown).

2 Buttercup
Outline of back-stitch (dark yellow), random cross-stitch filler (three shades of yellow); center is cross-stitch (pale green) with back-stitch shadow (tan); stamens cross-stitch (bright yellow broder). Stems cross-stitch (light green), leaves cross-stitch (darker shade of light green).

3 Ox-eye Daisy
Outlines back-stitch (pale grey-green), random cross-stitch filler, roughly in up-and-down rows ("shadow" stitches in slightly darker shades of grey-green). Center, three shades of yellow cross-stitch; stems also cross-stitch (dark and very dark-green border).

4 Clover
Large, double, irregular cross-stitch (two shades of light purple) with back-stitch accents (red). Leaves, back-stitch outlines, cross-stitch filler (dark green), markings (light grey-green) and stems (darker grey-green) cross-stitch.

5 Fleabane
The fine petals are rows of miniscule cross-stitches (two shades of pale lavender-pink); centers are random cross-stitches (two shades of yellow). Stems cross-stitches (light green).

6 Cinquefoil
Back-stitch outline (pale yellow), random cross-stitch filler (pale yellow), centers cross-stitch (light olive),

stamens cross-stitch (yellow), accents back-stitch (dark yellow), buds and stems random cross-stitches (three greens, broder thread), leaves back-stitch outline (olive), filler random cross-stitch (two shades of olive).

7 Blue-eyed grass
Very small random cross-stitches (bright light-blue), centers tiny random cross-stitches (yellow), back-stitch accent (dark blue), seedpods cross-stitch (olive), outlines back-stitch (brown). Leaves are random cross-stitches roughly in up-and-down rows (green), outlines back-stitch.

8 Ragged Robin
Back-stitch outlines (pink), random cross-stitch filler (pink), back-stitch accents (maroon), buds cross-stitch (grey-green) with back-stitch accents (maroon), stems cross-stitch (grey-green).

9 Pennyroyal
Outlines back-stitch (yellow), filler random cross-stitch (two shades of yellow), leaves outlined with back-stitch (dark green) and filled with random cross-stitches (dark green).

10 Golden Alexander
Individual cross-stitches (three shades of olive green), leaves back-stitch outlines (light green), filler random cross-stitches (olive-green broder).

11 Wild Strawberry
Back-stitch outline (white), random cross-stitch filler (white), center tiny random cross-stitches (two shades of yellow and two shades of olive green), leaves back-stitch outline (dark green), random cross-stitches filler (green), berries back-stitch outlines (dark red and pale green), random cross-stitch fillers (light and dark red and pale green and yellow).

12 Spurge
Cross-stitch (periwinkle blue, purple accents, maroon calyces), leaves cross-stitch (grey-green), back-stitch outlines (dark green), small leaves cross-stitch (light and dark green), runners (pale yellow green).

Ring of Roses Canvas Pillow

(old-fashioned roses) Cross-stitch crewel wool on bargello.

Redouté painted several lovely wreaths of roses; they have been reproduced and published in many ways through the years.

Bobbink & Atkins (now out of business, but once famous) was a nursery that among other things, specialized in old-fashioned roses. I believe that the small piece of one of Redouté's wreaths they used in their catalogs originally awakened my interest in the incredible old roses. Another of Redouté's wreaths was made up of all single roses, which gave me the inspiration for this pillow. It was only the inspiration, however; the choice of roses, both single and semidouble, was mine. All of the varieties are recognizable. The creamy white background proved just a bit too stark, so I added the red crosses, which are not cross-stitches at all but a group of backstitches in the shape of a cross.

This design was transferred from rough-sketch form directly to the bargello canvas, and then drawn in clearly with felt-tip pens in colors as close as possible to the colors to be used in the embroidery.

The yarn used was all Persian yarn; the needle was the usual short, dull-pointed, large-eyed one.

The embroidery was pressed on completion, and then made into the pillow.

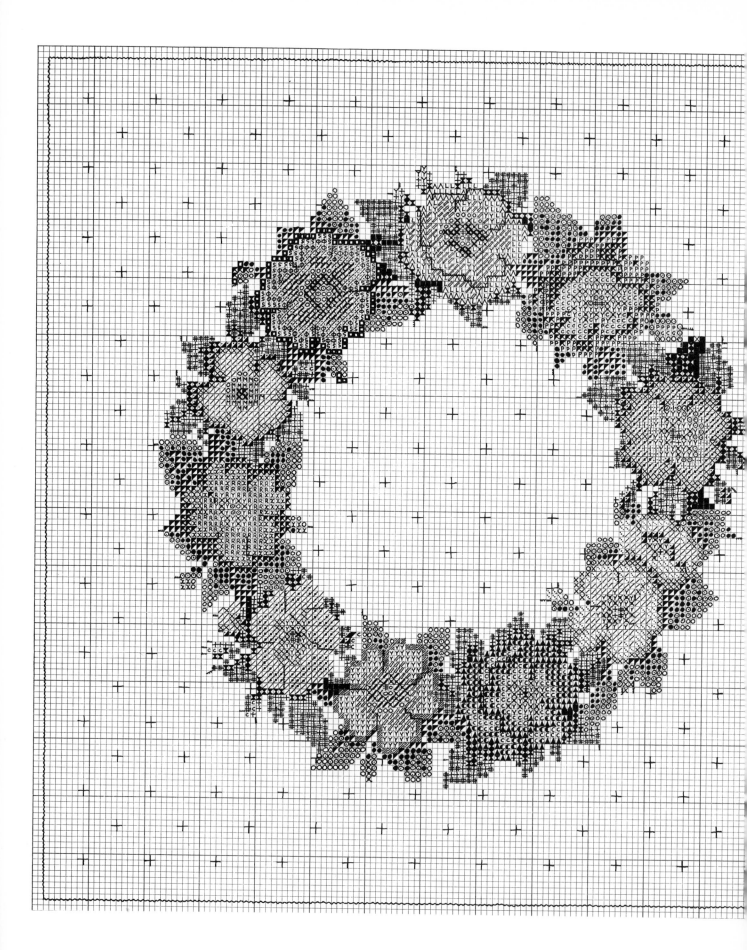

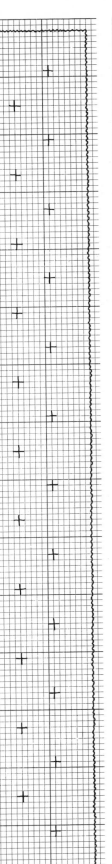

LEAVES	
■	DARKEST GREEN
▼	BLACK-GREEN
X	DARK GREEN
●	DARK OLIVE
+	MEDIUM GREEN
⊘	OLIVE GREEN
#	YELLOW-GREEN
O	WILLOW GREEN

ROSE 1	
▨	EGG YELLOW
Y	YELLOW
∕	LIGHT YELLOW
X	ORANGE-YELLOW
∕	LIGHT BURNT ORANGE
#	YELLOW-GREEN
O	WILLOW GREEN

ROSE 2	
∴	PALEST ROSE PINK
∕	PALE ROSE PINK
X	ROSE PINK
◢	MAGENTA
C	CHERRY RED
Y	YELLOW
X	ORANGE-YELLOW
#	YELLOW-GREEN

ROSE 3	
R	BRIGHT RED
X	MEDIUM DARK RED
◤	DARK RED
Y	YELLOW
X	ORANGE-YELLOW
⊘	OLIVE
O	WILLOW GREEN

ROSE 4	
◢	MAGENTA
X	ROSE PINK
∕	PALE ROSE PINK
M	MAROON
✕	DARK BURNT ORANGE
O	WILLOW GREEN

ROSE 5	
▣	DARK SALMON PINK
S	SALMON
●	ORANGE
∕	LIGHT ORANGE
✓	LIGHT SALMON
◢	PALE SALMON
X	ORANGE-YELLOW
✕	DARK BURNT ORANGE
⊘	OLIVE GREEN
O	WILLOW GREEN

ROSE 6	
∧	DARK LEMON YELLOW
L	LEMON YELLOW
Y	YELLOW
∕	LIGHT YELLOW
X	ORANGE-YELLOW
✕	DARK BURNT ORANGE
O	WILLOW GREEN
#	YELLOW-GREEN

ROSE 7	
P	PURPLE
◤	DARK RED
C	CHERRY RED
Y	YELLOW
X	ORANGE-YELLOW
⊘	OLIVE
+	MEDIUM GREEN

ROSE 8	
◢	MAGENTA
X	ROSE PINK
∕	PALEST ROSE PINK
I-	PALEST YELLOW
Y	YELLOW
∕	LIGHT ORANGE
X	ORANGE YELLOW
⊘	OLIVE
O	WILLOW GREEN

ROSE 9	
X	ROSE PINK
∴	LIGHT ROSE PINK
∕	PALE ROSE PINK
Y	YELLOW
X	ORANGE-YELLOW
#	YELLOW-GREEN
+	MEDIUM GREEN

ROSE 10	
▲	VERY DARK RED
◖	DARK CHERRY RED
C	CHERRY RED
Y	YELLOW
X	ORANGE-YELLOW
+	MEDIUM GREEN
I	DARK GREEN

Actual size: 16"x16".
Materials: bargello canvas. Crewel wool, Persian type.

It should be noted that many subtle variations of the coded colors were used for the flowers. All the leaf greens are the same, but they, too, could be varied.

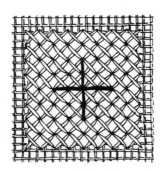

BACKGROUND	CREAM WHITE
+	CHERRY RED
___	INDICATES BACK-STITCH ACCENTS OF THE SAME COLOR AS THE NEAREST CROSS-STITCH, OR AS IN THE FLOWERS, THE DARKEST COLOR

Spring Bulb Flowers Tablecloth
D.M.C. six-strand cotton cross-stitch on deep-blue even-weave linen.

An oval-wreath design seemed most practical for this tablecloth. I actually was thinking of a round wreath to begin with. Somehow, round didn't seem so suitable for an oblong table. With an oval, enough room is left on both sides of the design to put a place setting. The material I had bought with a tablecloth in mind, and because it was the rare even-weave variety, I would have to use cross-stitch to take advantage of this. The bulb flowers just seemed right for a blue background; pictorially speaking only, however. The blue was a very potent color, and tended to kill the blue shades of the blue flowers. They seemed to just disappear into the background. So several of the blue flowers had to be changed to shades that would show up better. I suppose this could be considered embroiderer's license?

Also, counting dark-colored threads is quite difficult. I was warned about this when I bought the fabric, but I seldom believe such a thing until I experience it myself; it seems only fair for me to pass the warning on with the assurance that it is true: counting dark-colored threads is quite difficult!

The sketch was transferred to graph paper first, worked out on the graph paper in color next, and then transferred to the tablecloth in embroidery.

To save myself some counting while embroidering, I marked and basted all the guidelines I needed, as on page 65. This made it simple to do all the same color stitches at a time. All the tulip leaves are the same pale grey-green color; having all of them embroidered in the design made it easier to find where to start the next colors. Of course, one could start anywhere, but I think my way was rather expeditious.

The colors used were as close to the true flower colors as possible. Quite a bit of collecting of colors will be necessary to achieve the color variety used here. Fewer colors and shades could be used, of course, but I feel this would cause the design to lose some of its finesse. A 7" loop frame was used for this, which wasn't wholly necessary, but I wanted to keep the embroidery absolutely flat. The tablecloth was hemmed before starting the embroidery.

63

Actual size: tablecloth 60"x67"—embroidery
    25½"x21".
Materials: deep-blue even-weave linen, three strands
    D. M. C. six-strand cotton.

For this embroidery I used slightly different shades
whenever the same basic color was used. Using a
separate code for each would be impractical, so when a
code indicates light-blue, the light-blue in one flower
can be slightly varied from the light-blue in another
flower.

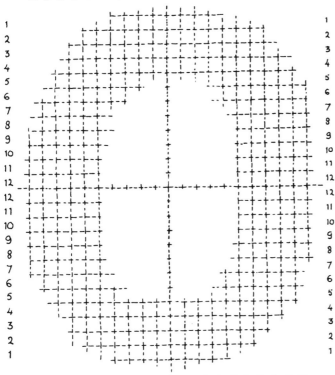

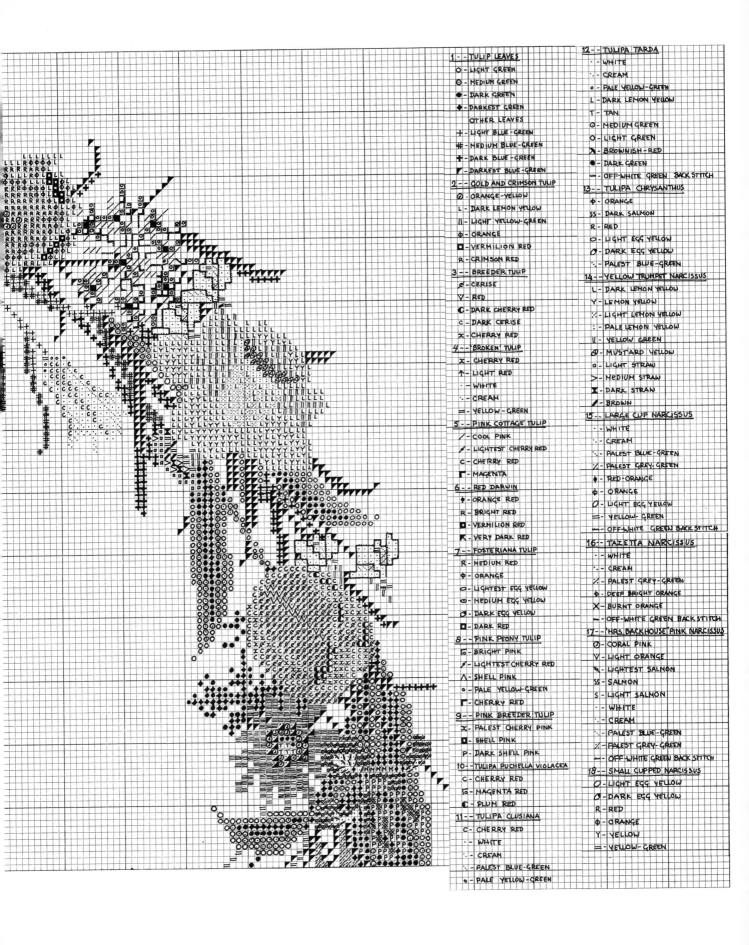

1-- TULIP LEAVES
- O - LIGHT GREEN
- O - MEDIUM GREEN
- ● - DARK GREEN
- ◆ - DARKEST GREEN

OTHER LEAVES
- + - LIGHT BLUE-GREEN
- ✚ - MEDIUM BLUE-GREEN
- ✚ - DARK BLUE-GREEN
- ◤ - DARKEST BLUE-GREEN

2-- GOLD AND CRIMSON TULIP
- 0 - ORANGE-YELLOW
- L - DARK LEMON YELLOW
- || - LIGHT YELLOW-GREEN
- φ - ORANGE
- ▣ - VERMILION RED
- R - CRIMSON RED

3-- BREEDER TULIP
- ɑ - CERISE
- V - RED
- C - DARK CHERRY RED
- c - DARK CERISE
- X - CHERRY RED

4-- BROKEN TULIP
- X - CHERRY RED
- ↑ - LIGHT RED
- ·· - WHITE
- ·· - CREAM
- = - YELLOW-GREEN

5-- PINK COTTAGE TULIP
- / - COOL PINK
- / - LIGHTEST CHERRY RED
- C - CHERRY RED
- Γ - MAGENTA

6-- RED DARWIN
- φ - ORANGE RED
- R - BRIGHT RED
- ▣ - VERMILION RED
- K - VERY DARK RED

7-- FOSTERIANA TULIP
- R - MEDIUM RED
- φ - ORANGE
- O - LIGHTEST EGG YELLOW
- O - MEDIUM EGG YELLOW
- O - DARK EGG YELLOW
- ▣ - DARK RED

8-- PINK PEONY TULIP
- ⓛ - BRIGHT PINK
- / - LIGHTEST CHERRY RED
- ∧ - SHELL PINK
- o - PALE YELLOW-GREEN
- Γ - CHERRY RED

9-- PINK BREEDER TULIP
- X - PALEST CHERRY PINK
- ▣ - SHELL PINK
- P - DARK SHELL PINK

10-- TULIPA PUCHELLA VIOLACEA
- C - CHERRY RED
- ⓛ - MAGENTA RED
- C - PLUM RED

11-- TULIPA CLUSIANA
- C - CHERRY RED
- ·· - WHITE
- ·· - CREAM
- ·· - PALEST BLUE-GREEN
- o - PALE YELLOW-GREEN

12-- TULIPA TARDA
- ·· - WHITE
- ·· - CREAM
- O - PALE YELLOW-GREEN
- L - DARK LEMON YELLOW
- T - TAN
- O - MEDIUM GREEN
- O - LIGHT GREEN
- ⟩ - BROWNISH-RED
- ● - DARK GREEN
- ⎯ - OFF-WHITE GREEN BACK STITCH

13-- TULIPA CHRYSANTHUS
- φ - ORANGE
- SS - DARK SALMON
- R - RED
- O - LIGHT EGG YELLOW
- O - DARK EGG YELLOW
- ·· - PALEST BLUE-GREEN

14-- YELLOW TRUMPET NARCISSUS
- L - DARK LEMON YELLOW
- Y - LEMON YELLOW
- ✕ - LIGHT LEMON YELLOW
- : - PALE LEMON YELLOW
- || - YELLOW GREEN
- ∅ - MUSTARD YELLOW
- ▫ - LIGHT STRAW
- > - MEDIUM STRAW
- X - DARK STRAW
- / - BROWN

15-- LARGE CUP NARCISSUS
- ·· - WHITE
- ·· - CREAM
- ·· - PALEST BLUE-GREEN
- ✕ - PALEST GREY-GREEN
- ◆ - RED-ORANGE
- φ - ORANGE
- O - LIGHT EGG YELLOW
- = - YELLOW-GREEN
- ⎯ - OFF-WHITE GREEN BACK STITCH

16-- TAZETTA NARCISSUS
- ·· - WHITE
- ·· - CREAM
- ✕ - PALEST GREY-GREEN
- ◆ - DEEP BRIGHT ORANGE
- X - BURNT ORANGE
- ⎯ - OFF-WHITE GREEN BACK STITCH

17-- 'MRS. BACKHOUSE' PINK NARCISSUS
- O - CORAL PINK
- V - LIGHT ORANGE
- ◣ - LIGHTEST SALMON
- SS - SALMON
- S - LIGHT SALMON
- ·· - WHITE
- ·· - CREAM
- ·· - PALEST BLUE-GREEN
- ✕ - PALEST GREY-GREEN
- ⎯ - OFF-WHITE GREEN BACK STITCH

18-- SMALL CUPPED NARCISSUS
- O - LIGHT EGG YELLOW
- O - DARK EGG YELLOW
- R - RED
- φ - ORANGE
- Y - YELLOW
- = - YELLOW-GREEN

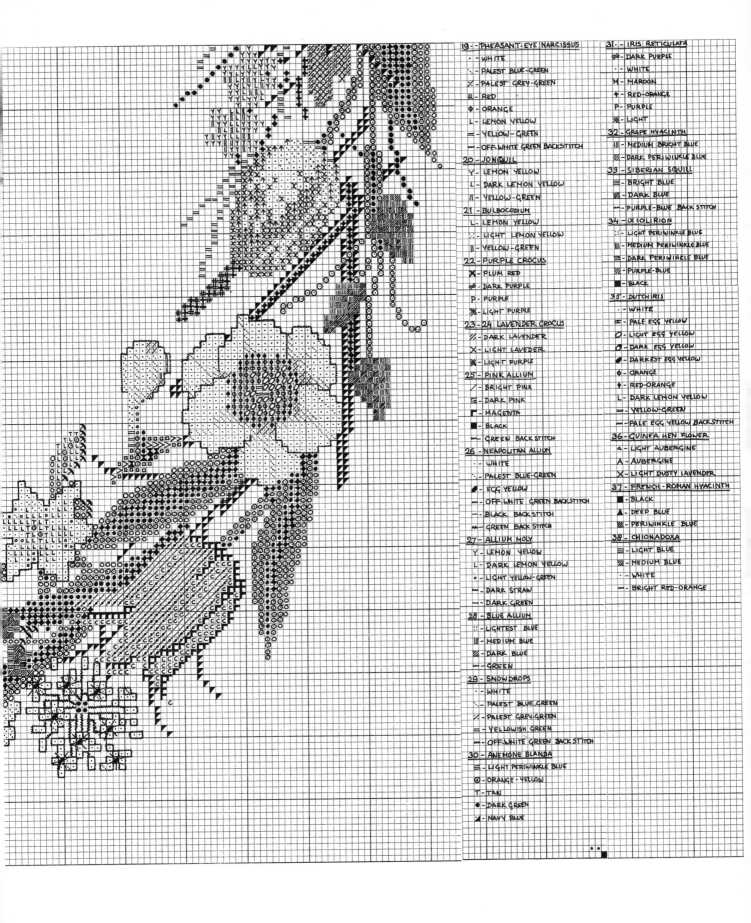

19 - - PHEASANT-EYE NARCISSUS
- · - WHITE
- : - PALEST BLUE-GREEN
- / - PALEST GREY-GREEN
- R - RED
- Φ - ORANGE
- L - LEMON YELLOW
- = - YELLOW-GREEN
- ~ - OFF-WHITE GREEN BACKSTITCH

20 - JONQUIL
- Y - LEMON YELLOW
- L - DARK LEMON YELLOW
- ‖ - YELLOW-GREEN

21 - BULBOCODIUM
- L - LEMON YELLOW
- : - LIGHT LEMON YELLOW
- ‖ - YELLOW-GREEN

22 - PURPLE CROCUS
- X - PLUM RED
- ∞ - DARK PURPLE
- P - PURPLE
- ✕ - LIGHT PURPLE

23-24 LAVENDER CROCUS
- ⁄⁄ - DARK LAVENDER
- X - LIGHT LAVENDER
- ✕ - LIGHT PURPLE

25 - PINK ALLIUM
- ⁄ - BRIGHT PINK
- ᴦ - DARK PINK
- Г - MAGENTA
- ■ - BLACK
- ~ - GREEN BACK STITCH

26 - NEAPOLITAN ALLIUM
- · - WHITE
- : - PALEST BLUE-GREEN
- ● - EGG YELLOW
- ~ - OFF-WHITE GREEN BACKSTITCH
- ~ - BLACK BACKSTITCH
- ~ - GREEN BACK STITCH

27 - ALLIUM MOLY
- Y - LEMON YELLOW
- L - DARK LEMON YELLOW
- o - LIGHT YELLOW-GREEN
- ~ - DARK STRAW
- - - DARK GREEN

28 - BLUE ALLIUM
- :: - LIGHTEST BLUE
- ‖ - MEDIUM BLUE
- ⁄⁄ - DARK BLUE
- - - GREEN

29 - SNOWDROPS
- · - WHITE
- : - PALEST BLUE-GREEN
- / - PALEST GREY-GREEN
- = - YELLOWISH GREEN
- ~ - OFF-WHITE GREEN BACK STITCH

30 - ANEMONE BLANDA
- ≡ - LIGHT PERIWINKLE BLUE
- ⊙ - ORANGE-YELLOW
- T - TAN
- ● - DARK GREEN
- ✕ - NAVY BLUE

31 - - IRIS RETICULATA
- ∞ - DARK PURPLE
- · - WHITE
- M - MAROON
- ✦ - RED-ORANGE
- P - PURPLE
- ✕ - LIGHT

32 - GRAPE HYACINTH
- ‖ - MEDIUM BRIGHT BLUE
- ⁄⁄ - DARK PERIWINKLE BLUE

33 - SIBERIAN SQUILL
- ≡ - BRIGHT BLUE
- ⁄⁄ - DARK BLUE
- ~ - PURPLE-BLUE BACK STITCH

34 - IXIOLIRION
- : - LIGHT PERIWINKLE BLUE
- ‖ - MEDIUM PERIWINKLE BLUE
- ≡ - DARK PERIWINKLE BLUE
- ⁄⁄ - PURPLE-BLUE
- ■ - BLACK

35 - DUTCH IRIS
- · - WHITE
- ≖ - PALE EGG YELLOW
- O - LIGHT EGG YELLOW
- Ø - DARK EGG YELLOW
- ∅ - DARKEST EGG YELLOW
- Φ - ORANGE
- ✦ - RED-ORANGE
- L - DARK LEMON YELLOW
- = - YELLOW-GREEN
- ~ - PALE EGG YELLOW BACKSTITCH

36 - GUINEA HEN FLOWER
- a - LIGHT AUBERGINE
- A - AUBERGINE
- X - LIGHT DUSTY LAVENDER

37 - FRENCH-ROMAN HYACINTH
- ■ - BLACK
- ▲ - DEEP BLUE
- ⁄⁄ - PERIWINKLE BLUE

38 - CHIONADOXA
- ≡ - LIGHT BLUE
- ⁄⁄ - MEDIUM BLUE
- · - WHITE
- ~ - BRIGHT RED-ORANGE

Peace Rose Place Mat

D.M.C. six-strand cotton thread on coarse Danish even-weave linen.

Peace rose could be copied and embroidered from my design with little effort and time. It occurred to me that somebody might embroider place mats for a special occasion; making several of the same design wouldn't take too long. Other roses could be made following the same design, but using other colors. As to their names, however, I would have no guarantee that there is another rose with the same shape as Peace!

Actual size: place mat 12¼"x16¼", flower 5¼"x4¼".

Materials: white Danish linen (20 threads to the inch), four strands D. M. C. six-strand cotton.

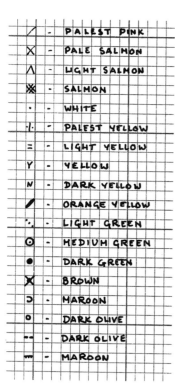

∕	-	PALEST PINK
X	-	PALE SALMON
Λ	-	LIGHT SALMON
※	-	SALMON
·	-	WHITE
·|·	-	PALEST YELLOW
=	-	LIGHT YELLOW
Y	-	YELLOW
N	-	DARK YELLOW
∕	-	ORANGE YELLOW
·.·	-	LIGHT GREEN
⊙	-	MEDIUM GREEN
●	-	DARK GREEN
✕	-	BROWN
⊃	-	MAROON
◖	-	DARK OLIVE
··	-	DARK OLIVE
ˉˉ	-	MAROON

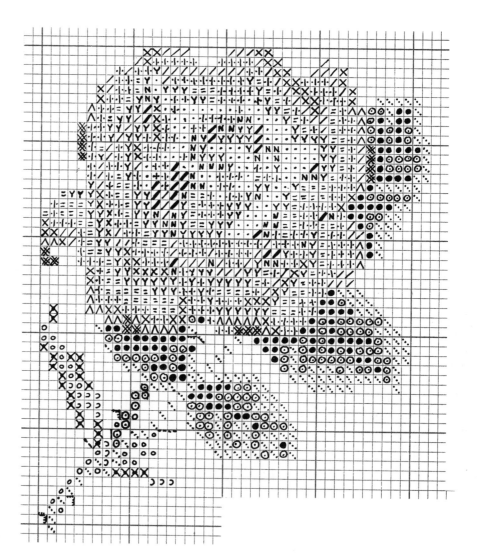

The design was first sketched on tracing paper, then transferred to graph paper, colored in, and then embroidered on an already edged and hemmed place mat. A very simple edging stitch seems appropriate. I didn't use a frame for this, but a 4″ one might be helpful to some.

Flowers Embroidered in Various Materials

This chapter is meant to suggest how to go about making imaginative use of all sorts of materials and stitches to make realistic-looking flowers and other plant materials.

Again, for those who collect, finding helpful items for this type of embroidery is not difficult. For the two pieces described in this chapter, only small amounts of each material were needed. It probably is possible to find all the things mentioned here, but how and where is difficult to say. Let inspiration suggest how to depict a certain item, and then try to find some kind of fabric or thread or snippet of leather that will be suitable for use in the embroidery. It certainly would be possible to work the same subject in more than one way and with different combinations of materials than the ones I used.

Mixed Fall Bouquet

Included are wool, cotton, and silk thread. Many kinds of stitches and methods such as appliqué, quilting, and tambour work, using many items such as beads and raffia to achieve special effects.

In a piece such as this, one's imagination can go wild. Anything goes! I tried to give as many ideas as I could; here again, the possibilities are numerous.

The design was vague in my mind, and only the basic design was drawn on the canvas. A rough sketch was made and used as a guide while I embroidered. My readers will have an easier time than I had when they try making this embroidery!

The background material is a linen canvas often used for crewel work (actually painter's canvas) because it had a medium texture and neutral shade, and would therefore blend well with any texture and any color. This embroidery was stretched on the frame before the work was started.

Actual size: embroidery 9"x12", frame 12"x16".

Materials: Those used for this embroidery are numerous and will be described separately with each subject. The background is painter's canvas (linen).

1 Yarrow "gold cup"
The many small flowers are made with three strands of D. M. C. six-strand cotton (yellow) in buttonhole stitch for the petals. The centers are crewel wool French knots (two twists each) in a slightly greener yellow than the petals. I didn't count how many florets in this umbel, but there must be hundreds! The stem is made of two rows of back-stitch with a row of chain-stitch in between. Two strands of light grey-green D. M. C. six-strand cotton were used for the stem.

2 Sugar Maple leaves
These leaves are only unusual in their color. The outlines are buttonhole stitch, the filler satin stitch, and the veins stem-stitch. There are eighteen shades of yellow, orange, and red, some of the shade variants barely discernible, but the total giving a rich brilliance which is as close to the real thing as I can get.

3 Milk weed pods and seeds
The pods are made of quilted appliqué. The fabrics are grey-green organdy over grey-green curtain shantung silk. The thread two shades of light green single strand D. M. C. six-strand. The stem couched crewel wool. The couching done with light-green D. M. C. six-strand. The heavy parts of the seeds are made with two shades of brown D. M. C. six-strand (three-strands) in buttonhole stitch with satin stitch centers. The thin fibers (flyers) are made of split silk buttonhole twist.

4 Curly dock
The stem is made up of stem-stitch in dark-brown, three strands of D. M. C. six-strand cotton. The seed pods (again hundreds of them) are small lazy-daisy stitches made of very dark brown D. M. C., using the full six strands with orange accents in each center.

5 Honesty
Each pod is made by sewing two layers of white China silk together, and overcasting (and then trimming) the outlines. The close overcasting is done with taupe single-strand D. M. C. The seeds are embroidered on the under layer of silk before joining. They are satin stitch—dark taupe silk buttonhole twist. The veins are the same single-strand D. M. C. as the outlines done in double-running stitch. The resulting "silver dollars" are tacked to the background at the tips. The stems are tightly couched stem-stitch.

6 "Rugosa" rose-hips
These consist of stuffed appliqué of bright red China silk with dried-up calyx of six-strand D. M. C. The stitch I used here has no name as far as I know, so it is best described as woven picot, maybe, better, fantasy woven picot. The leaves are appliqué dark green felt with the appliqué stitches spaced to serve as serrations of the leaves, the veins back-stitches. The stem and thorns are a random collection of back-stitches.

7 Tansy
The individual florets are made of turkey stitches of yellow crewel wool. The stems and leaves are dark-green, two strands of D. M. C. The stitches are back-stitch, lazy-daisy, and chain-stitch.

8 Bayberry
The twig is brown crewel wool closely couched with grey D. M. C., letting bits of the wool "peek" through the grey thread. The berries are padded satin-stitch, antique grey silk (over 100 years old).

9 Ornamental grass
This is made of light-straw-colored D. M. C. thread, the the stitches are lazy-daisies.

10 Boxwood
The front-side leaves are dark-green D. M. C. satin stitch. The back-side leaves are light-green border-thread satin stitch and stem-stitch with dark-green buttonhole stitch edges.

11 Ornamental grass
The small stars are made of lazy-daisy stitches of dark-brown D. M. C. with yellow open lazy-daisy centers.

12 Agrostis grass
Each little hull is made of D. M. C. lavender single-thread D. M. C. double lazy-daisy stitches.

13 Ornamental grass Briza
This is also a grouping of lazy-daisy stitches in a straw-color D. M. C. Each "pod" has a yoke of dark straw-brown D. M. C. made of lazy-daisy stitches.

14 Strawflower
Made of red imitation raffia loop stitches. The center is turkey stitch in yellow crewel wool. The stem is green D. M. C.

15 Oats
The natural raffia seems ideal for this subject. For the finer parts, the raffia was split to the desired thinness.

16 Ammobium
The flowers are white imitation raffia in loop stitches. The center is yellow crewel-wool turkey-stitch. The stems are all green D. M. C. in buttonhole stitch.

17 Briza grass
The pods are a combination of lavender-tan D. M. C. lazy-daisy stitches and buttonhole stitches.

18 Mistletoe
The leaves are two shades of grey-green silk appliquéd and quilted. The blossoms are miniscule French knots, the berries grey-green silk-covered beads.

19 Bayberry
The Fall colors of the foliage are easily made with many shades of orange, red, and pink. Buttonhole stitch outlines and satin-stitch filler. The berries are lacquered wooden beads sewn to the canvas with black crewel wool. The stem is closely couched stem-stitch in brown D. M. C.

African Violets Picture
Wool and D.M.C. six-strand cotton threads.

African violets come in many shapes, and can have neat straight-edged petals or very frilly ones with tips of pale green or frosted, wavy edges. It would be impossible to make an embroidery including all types, of course, so I picked a small collection from a cover design I made for *Flower Grower*. Using just one or two flowers and a bud of a type seemed sufficient to indicate the variety. All the flowers are worked in D.M.C. six-strand cotton.

The leaves that I intended to embroider in a plushy stitch seemed ideal for Turkey work. I used the stitch at random, first following the leaf edges, and then filling in with stitches as tightly packed as possible. This made a pile so snug that, after being trimmed and shaped, it could be washed and ironed without damage.

The background is ecru-colored hardänger, a soft, even-weave fabric. In this case the even weave was of no consequence, but the soft touch and color seemed very suitable to bring out the contrasting flowers and leaves. A small hand-hoop frame was used to keep the embroidery stretched while it was being worked.

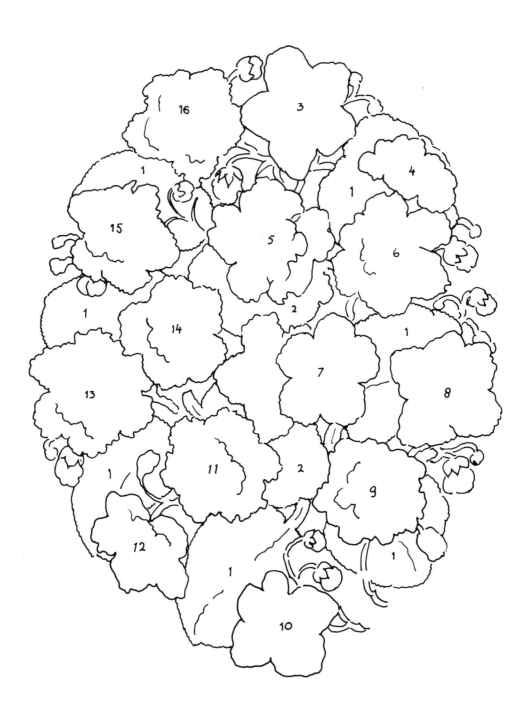

Actual size: 6¼"x4¾".

Materials: Hardanger. Flowers two strands D. M. C. six-strand cotton except where stated otherwise. Leaves crewel wool, mostly Persian type.

1 Turkey stitch, very tightly packed. Light green around the edges of each leaf and along the veins. Dark-green filler. Clipped and shaped with very sharp embroidery scissors.

2 Turkey stitch, same as #1, but using two darker shades of green.

3 Buttonhole stitch outlines (magenta) satin-stitch filler. Over-hand stitch around edges of petals (white single strand).

4 Buttonhole stitch outlines (palest lavender) satin stitch filler (two shades of lavender).

5 Buttonhole stitch outlines (lavender), satin-stitch filler (two darker shades of lavender).

6 Buttonhole stitch outlines (light purple), satin-stitch filler (light purple, deep blue, and dark purple).

7 Buttonhole stitch outlines (pink), satin-stitch filler (two lighter shades of pink).

8 Buttonhole stitch outlines (dark red), satin-stitch filler (dark red and purple) single-strand buttonhole stitch around edges (yellow).

9 Buttonhole stitch outlines (white) satin-stitch filler (palest yellow and pale yellow-green).

10 Buttonhole stitch outlines (light magenta), satin-stitch filler (light red) and throat (light yellow-green).

11 Buttonhole stitch outlines (pink), satin-stitch filler (darker pink and dark red), single-strand buttonhole stitch fringe along edges (light yellow-green).

12 Buttonhole stitch outlines (purple), satin-stitch filler (dark and darkest purple).

13 Buttonhole stitch outlines (palest pink), satin-stitch filler (two shades pale pink).

14 Buttonhole stitch outlines (deep periwinkle blue), satin-stitch filler (two shades darker periwinkle blue).

15 Buttonhole stitch outlines (lavender), satin-stitch filler (three shades of lighter lavender).

16 Buttonhole stitch outlines (deep blue, lighter than #14), satin-stitch filler (deep blue and purple).

All stems are light-green overcast crewel wool. All calyxes light green. Bud (petal part) next to 6 is lavender; above 8, pink; next to 9, light green; above 10, pink and light green; below 13, light green; near 15, lavender; below 16, deep blue; above 16, light green. All in two strands D. M. C. All stamens are yellow bullion knots.

Species List

Page 55, **Field Flowers**
    Orange Hawkweed, *Hieriacum aurantiacum*
    Buttercup, *Ranunculus acris*
    Ox-eye daisy, *Chrysanthemum leucanthemum*
    Red clover, *Trifolium pratense*
    Fleabane, *Erigeron philadelphicus*
    Cinquefoil, *Potentilla recta*
    Blue-eyed grass, *Sisyrinchium angustifolium*
    Ragged robin, *Lychnis flos-cuculi*
    Penny royal, *Lysimachia nummularia*
    Golden alexander, *Zizia aurea*
    Wild strawberry, *Fragaria virginiana*
    Vetch, *Vicia cracca*

Page 58, **Ring of Roses**
    Rosa gallica
    Rosa damascena
    Rosa muscosa
    Rosa eglanteria
    Rosa florabunda

Page 63, **Bulb Flowers Tablecloth**
    Tulip, *Tulipa* 'Darwin'
    Tulip, *Tulipa* 'Broken'
    Tulip, 'Marietta'
    Tulip, 'De Wet'
    Tulip, *Tulipa fosteriana*
    Tulip, 'Peach Blossom'
    Tulip, 'Aristocrat'
    Tulip, *Tulipa violacaea*
    Tulip, *Tulipa clusiana*
    Tulip, *Tulipa tarda*
    Tulip, *Tulipa kolpakowskiana*
    Daffodil, Narcissus 'King Alfred'
    Narcissus, 'Orange bride'
    Narcissus, *N. tazetta* 'geranium'
    Narcissus, *N. tazetta* 'geranium'
    Daffodil, 'Mrs. R. O. Backhouse'
    Narcissus, 'Edward Buxton'
    Narcissus, *N. poeticus*
    Narcissus, *N. jonquilla*
    Narcissus, *N. cyclameneus*
    Crocus, 'Paulus Potter'

Crocus, 'Remembrance'
Allium, *A. ostrowskyanum*
Allium, *A. neapolitanum*
Allium, *A. moly*
Allium, *A. caeruleum*
Snowdrop, *Galanthus nivalis*
Anemone, *Anemone blanda*
Iris, *Iris reticulata*
Grape hyacinth, *Muscari*
Scilla, *S. siberica*
Ixiolirion, *I. montanum*
Iris, *I. xiphium praecox* 'Princess Irene'
Guinea flower, *Fritillaria meleagris*
French hyacinth, *Hyacinthus orientalis*
Chionadoxa, *C. lucilae*

Page 70, **Rose Place Mat**
    Hybrid tea rose 'Peace,' *Rosa odorata hybrida*

Page 72, **Fall Bouquet**
    Yarrow 'Gold plate,' *Achillea filipendulina*
    Sugar maple leaves, *Acer saccharum*
    Milk-weed pods and seeds, *Asclepias syriaca*
    Curly dock, *Rumex crispus*
    Honesty, *Lunaria biennis*
    Rose hips, *Rosa rugosa*
    Tansy, *Tanacetum vulgare*
    Bayberry, *Myrica cerifera*
    Ornamental grass, *Glyceria aquatica*
    Ornamental grass, *Luzula pilosa*
    Boxwood, *Buxus sempervirens*
    Agrostis grass, *Agrostis palustris*
    Ornamental grass, *Briza maxima*
    Strawflower, *Helichrysum bracteatum*
    Oats, *Avena sativa*
    Ammobium, *Ammobium*
    Briza grass, *Briza minor*
    Mistletoe, *Viscum album*
    Bayberry, *Myrica pennsylvanica*

Page 76, **African Violets**
    Saint-paulia

Bibliography

Following are the names of books and magazines which provide excellent sources for ideas, research, and stitches. All of the books and magazines and artworks listed here have been useful to me at one time or another.

Ornamente der Volkskunst, Bossert
Verlag Ernst Wasmuth, Tübingen, West Germany
Embroidered Folk designs

The Concise British Flora in Colour, W. Keble Martin
Holt, Rinehart and Winston, New York

Gerda Bengtsson's Book of Danish Stitchery
Van Nostrand Reinhold, New York

Wild Green Things in the City, Anne Ophelia Dowden
The Thomas Y. Crowell Co., New York

Handbook of Stitches, Grete Peterson and Elsie Svennas
A small and unpretentious book containing a gold mine of stitches. I always keep this booklet handy.

100 Embroidery Stitches, Book No. 150, Coates and Clark
(Distributed by Scribners, New York)

The D. M. C. Ethnic Stitchery Books

*Wild Flowers to Know and Grow, Jean Hersey
Van Nostrand, New York

Wild Flowers, Homer D. House
The Macmillan Company, New York
Still one of the best, if not the best, of the wild flower books. Here one can find many wild flowers depicted in such a way as to be suggestive of natural design.

Handbook of Paisleys, American Fabrics

Great Tapestries, Joseph Jobe
Edita S. A., Lausanne, Switzerland

Woman's Day Book of American Needlework, Rose Wilder Lane
Simon and Schuster, New York

*Dutch Still-life Painting in the Seventeenth Century, Ingvar Bergström
Thomas Yoseloff, New York

*Book of Wild Flowers, First and Second Series, Elsa Felsko
Thomas Yoseloff, New York

*The American Gardener's Book of Bulbs, T. H. Everett
Random House, New York

*The Complete Guide to Bulbs, Patrick M. Synge
E. P. Dutton and Co., New York

Oxford Book of Wild Flowers, S. Ary and M. Gregoris
Oxford University Press, New York

Hardy Perennials, Frances Perry
E. P. Dutton and Co., New York

Cross Stitch Embroidery II, Gerda Bengtsson
Haandarbejdets Fremmes Forlag, Copenhagen, Denmark

Pulled Thread Work, Esther Fangel
Haandarbejdets Fremmes Forlag, Copenhagen, Denmark

Flowers: The Flower Piece in European Painting, Margaretta Salinger
Harper and Brothers, New York

Painted and Printed Fabrics, Henri Clouzot and Frances Morris
Metropolitan Museum of Art, New York

Encyclopedia of Roses, H. Edland
St. Martin's Press, New York

Paintings by Botticelli, Renoir, Van Gogh, Early Dutch Painters, and others
Various Garden Magazines and Catalogs

* Out of print, but should be available at public libraries.

Materials

Fabrics

For Cross Stitch
Even weave linen in many gauges and occasionally in colors (red, blue, light blue, yellow or ecru). Switzerland and Denmark are the main suppliers.
Hardänger, usually in white and ecru, but sometimes in colors.
Open mesh canvas of various sorts and gauges.

For Cotton or Linen Needlework (uneven weave fabrics)
Huck Toweling
Diapercloth (bird's eye)
Burlap
Belgian and Irish linen
Painter's Canvas

For Backgrounds for Crewel Work, etc.
Velvet or Velveteen (dress or upholsterer's varieties)
Unclipped velvet
Suede Cloth
Dress or upholsterer's linen
Dress or suiting materials with slight or no texture or design (no prints)

For Open Work
Loose weave linens or cotton
Loose weave combination fabrics
Loose even weave linens

Threads

Woolen

Crewel and Persian yarn, some knitting yarns; fingering yarn is useful for fine woolen embroidery

Cotton

D. M. C. has by far the greatest color selection of 6 strand embroidery floss. They also carry pearl floss. The Danish embroidery floss comes in a rather limited range of colors, but most are very good floral colors, useful for subdued effects because the thread is not mercerized.

Silk and Linen

Both are hard to find but worth looking for when special effects are wanted. Linen thread is particularly suited to open and lace work.

Sources

The Parson's Wife, Lisbon, New Hampshire 03585
Hanover Needlecraft, Hanover, New Hampshire 03755
Boutique Margot, 26 West 54th Street, New York, New York 10019
Clara Waever, Ostergade 42, Copenhagen, Denmark
The Needlewoman Ltd., 146 Regent Street, London, W.1 England
Alice Maynard, 724 Fifth Avenue, New York, New York 10019
Merribbee, 209 West Lancaster, Fort Worth, Texas 76107
5 and 10¢ stores
Dress making and notion shops
Sewing centers
Upholstery sales places
Mill end outlets
Arts and crafts stores

There are many more sources than mentioned here, but these are all stores which served me personally at one time or another. The above mentioned do not necessarily carry everything one might need for a given piece of embroidery, but usually one can collect most items in a few of these places.